Royal Academy of Dancing

BALLET
Class

Royal Academy of Dancing

BALLET *Class*

Foreword by Dame Margot Fonteyn de Arias

EBURY
PRESS

Published by Ebury Press
National Magazine House
72 Broadwick Street
London W1V 2BP

First impression 1984

Edited and designed by Swallow Books
32 Hermes Street, London N1

The Royal Academy of Dancing would like to
thank the teachers and examiners who
contributed to the preparation of this book, in
particular, Susan Danby LRAD, ARAD.

Managing Editor: **Sarah Snape**
Editor: **Loulou Brown**
Editorial assistant: **Angie Doran**
Art Director: **David Young**
Designer: **Gill Della Casa**
Assistant designers: **Lynn Hector
and Howard Selina**
Studio: **Del and Co**
Illustrator: **Coral Mula**
Articles: **Craig Dodd**
Colour photography:
**Darryl Williams, The Dance Library
and Jesse Davis, Mike Davis Studios**
Black and white photography:
Bill Cooper, Chris Davies and Barry Lewis
Reference photography: **Bill Cooper**

ISBN 0 85223 358 2

Photoset by Wagstaff Design Associates
Origination by Rainbow Reproductions
Printed and bound in Italy by New Interlitho Spa

CONTENTS

FOREWORD
BY
DAME MARGOT FONTEYN DE ARIAS

I have always thought of dance as being magic in many ways, both for those who get their enjoyment out of watching it and for those who live and work in this special world.

This book is a wonderful guide for anyone wanting to know more about the world of dance, especially students, no matter what course they are following. The many drawings included will be a useful addition to regular study and will add to your knowledge of the technique of ballet. They won't teach you how to dance — that is strictly for your teacher — but they will help you to understand the pace at which you should work, in particular, the correct time in your studies to advance to more difficult steps. It is very important that you should not be in too much of a hurry and overstretch yourself, as then there will almost certainly be problems in the future.

I think it is very important also to realize the true value of examinations and certificates, which are not necessarily the passport to a place in a company. If a young student achieves high marks it does not mean she or he is going to be a prospective ballerina or *danseur noble*, but it might suggest that it is worth considering moving on to serious study. I always think that a young child with high marks is like a big fish in a small pond but that a child as a serious student may only become like a little fish in the ocean!

If you are just dancing for your own enjoyment and satisfaction, if you are learning and hoping that one day you will dance on a stage for the enjoyment and satisfaction of others, or if you are just watching and appreciating dance, I hope that this book will be a marvellous guide for you to the magic world of dance.

Margot Fonteyn de Arias

A DAY IN THE LIFE OF
ERROL PICKFORD
STUDENT AT THE ROYAL BALLET SCHOOL

I'd like to be a Principal Dancer of the Royal Ballet or American Ballet Theater. It's aiming high when you think that I didn't start out as a dancer, and sometimes I still wake up and wonder what I'm doing.

I was seven when I started doing gymnastics at my primary school in my home town of Stoke-on-Trent. Our team was very good, and I carried on until I was ten. Then somebody said that we could give it more quality if we went to ballet classes. So I ended up doing that once a week. I was the only boy and felt very self-conscious. I felt that I was just doing class as everyone else wanted me to. I didn't even tell my classmates in school till I was twelve. Sometimes I hated it.

Then at twelve I became a bit more used to ballet and my mother and my ballet teacher, who I liked, suggested that I should go to the Hammond School in Chester. I was at the Hammond for five years. I would finish my classes at the comprehensive at 4pm, then go to Hammond, have a snack and then do ballet till about 6 or 6.30pm. Then all day Saturday I'd do ballet, too, sometimes till 8 or 9pm, if we were near exams.

At the comprehensive I got on all right with most of my class, but there was the usual teasing about tights and all that sort of thing. It wasn't too bad, especially as I was so good at sports. There were about twelve boys from the Hammond there, but as we were all different ages we didn't stick around together.

I was always best at sports, and never liked the ordinary subjects. I was so keen on physical activities

that I even thought of going into the army or the marines at one time. But by the time I was fourteen I knew I showed promise at dancing and that it was the thing I could do best. I even started to work at being the best in my class and come out top. And I did! By now I was in my last year at school and decided that ballet wasn't so bad after all. I suppose I was getting better at it. I was lucky to get the Phyllis Bedells Bursary, which paid for me to go to London to work for my Advanced Ballet exams. I was also awarded a second scholarship, the Paul Clarke Scholarship, and was given a small part in the film *Death in Venice*, which paid for me to go for four weeks to the Ilkley Summer School. Once you decide to take dance seriously you have to work hard at it all the time, even in the holidays.

When I was sixteen I auditioned for the Royal Ballet School and was lucky enough to be accepted. I was very flattered to be put into the second-year class straight away.

It's been fantastic here. Not just for the teaching but because I've had the opportunity to do other things, like dance in the Royal Variety Show. I remember I was very pleased to be given the chance to appear in a Gala, but unfortunately, I fell flat on my back. It was partly the orchestra's fault really as they were going too fast and the stage was a bit slippery, although I believe it had been washed down before with coke to make it more sticky, a trick often used in theatres. Anyway I just got up and carried on. My teacher said it was the first time he had seen me smile during the performance! In

1983 I tried for the Adeline Genée Medal Awards and won the Silver medal and £1000.

We have a full day at the school with many different classes to do. I get up at about 7am with the help of an alarm clock. I have a light breakfast and then I wash my hair and sort out my dance clothes, which I will have washed the night before. Then on to my bike and off to the school which takes about ten minutes. Once there – around 8.20am – I change and do a bit of work by myself in the studio to get warm and wake myself up. When I'm warm I can take off my woollen leg warmers. Well, they have to come off anyway as the school is strict about what we wear for class.

I have favourite things I like doing in class. Most of what we do is the regular ballet class any student knows about, but I particularly like doing *pirouettes* and *tours*. I think they're my best steps. I work hard at the *adage*, with lots of stretching and bending as I want to get my legs higher. It's not that they're bad; it's just that I want them to look better.

Class finishes about 10.30am and then we have a half hour break. Sometimes I'll have a yoghurt but I never seem to get the flavour I want. I always end up with cherry.

After the break we have different classes depending on the day. One day it might be Virtuosity, which is for boys to build up stamina and their special virtuoso steps. Another day we might have a contemporary dance class which I enjoy as it's free and relaxing. We might have a period of coaching when we have a chance to see ourselves on video

which can be horrible. You think you are doing a fantastic turn and then look and see that your bottom was sticking right out! *Pas de deux* classes are hard work, especially as we sometimes have to partner two girls. There are only 12 boys in my *pas de deux* class and far more girls. It's not the size of the girl that counts. A big girl might look heavy, but she will know how to help do a lift. A small girl might just stand there, so that you have to heave her up into the air.

We also have Mime classes. I like these classes, but at first I felt a little embarassed trying to show 'evil', 'romance' or 'comedy' in front of my friends. Boys have to mime such roles as court gentlemen while the girls are peasants, or we have to work on the role of the evil witch, Carabosse, from *The Sleeping Beauty*.

Later in the day we will have a period of rehearsing a ballet, perhaps something we are going to do in a Gala or for the school performance

at Covent Garden. I like this best as it's the nearest we get to being like professional dancers.

The school day ends around 6.30 to 7pm, and after a quick shower and change I'm on my bike and back home. I don't do much on weekday evenings as I am always so tired. Just a quick meal, something simple as I'm hopeless at cooking. Fortunately my flatmate, also from school, is brilliant at it. We have to do all our shopping in one big go at the weekends as there is hardly time to get out of the school during the day. I might do a bit of tidying up, wash the pile of wet ballet clothes, watch a bit of television and that's it before bed, sometimes as early as 9pm.

Weekends are different as we go out and stay with friends to get away from school and ballet for a time. After a break like this I can look forward to Monday mornings back at school.

Considering that I started out without any real interest in classical

ballet I really like it now. I look forward to being able to do the big exciting things like *Le Corsaire pas de deux*. I've got a video of Baryshnikov doing it. He's my favourite dancer and I think he's brilliant. I don't have to decide about joining a company for a while yet. I'm only seventeen and I have to finish my training at the Royal Ballet School, and have a go at the Genée Awards for a second time, as I am still young enough to compete. If I'm accepted into the Royal Ballet I'd like to work my way up from the Corps de Ballet to Soloist and then Principal.

I haven't thought much about work outside the classical ballet. I don't feel I'd make much of a choreographer, but one day I might like to have a try at something more commercial, like Wayne Sleep's company DASH. I'd love to dance in a musical, but I don't think I ever will as I can't sing. Not at the moment, anyway.

A DAY IN THE LIFE OF
RAVENNA TUCKER
PRINCIPAL DANCER WITH THE ROYAL BALLET

When I was young in Hong Kong, I never dreamed that one day I would stand on the stage of the Royal Opera House under a shower of lovely daffodils, having danced in the same performance of *La Bayadere* as Rudolph Nureyev.

I was born in Malaysia in 1962, but my family moved to Hong Kong when I was 7 and I started ballet classes there. I only had one a week, on Friday after school. I started doing an extra class when I was eight, which meant my father had to drive me quite a way to the studio, but I was still not thinking of dancing as a career. Our teacher did not push or bully us, but she did encourage our talents even though she knew most of us were there just because dancing was a hobby.

There wasn't much chance to see ballet in Hong Kong. I knew all about Nureyev and Margot Fonteyn, Antoinette Sibley and Anthony Dowell, but I only saw the Stuttgart Ballet and a group of dancers John Field brought over, including Doreen Wells. Elaine MacDonald of the Scottish Ballet came over to do *Swan Lake*. Then I knew I wanted to be a ballerina like her, though I had already danced in the *corps* of *Swan Lake* myself in a local theatre, aged eleven!

By the age of thirteen I had passed all the ballet exams I had taken and was thinking of taking it up seriously. During my parent's leave in Britain I was able to attend RAD Summer School to find out what ballet was really like. After that, I rang my father and told him I wanted to be a dancer.

I was now fifteen and went back to Hong Kong to carry on with my ordinary schooling. I did my best, as my parents thought I should get some qualifications because so many things can go wrong with a dancing career. It's good to have something to fall back on. But by this time I had become determined to be a dancer, and I applied to the Royal Ballet School and entered the annual Adeline Genée competition in London.

I came from Hong Kong to London for the competition with two other girls. The parents at our school clubbed together to pay our fares and expenses. We were coached in the set class, and in spite of the cold and dreary weather and feeling homesick, we enjoyed the work and we cheered up a bit when our teacher came over to see us. There were about seventeen competitors and we all had to do the set class, and then our variations, in front of Merle Park, Phyllis Bedells and Peter Schaufuss who were the judges. I certainly didn't expect to win. When it was announced that I had won I was absolutely thrilled, I really was. The prize was the Gold Medal, £100 and a place (not a scholarship) at the Royal Ballet School.

I went back to Hong Kong to finish my 'O' levels and set off for London again to take up my place at the Royal Ballet School. I cried at the airport, but felt happier when I met three lovely Australian girls there. They were crying, too! Once we got to London we didn't have much time to be miserable. There were so many different classes – character, modern, repertoire – all new to me. I did my first performance with the

school at the Opera House. We danced *Checkmate Concerto* and *Sinfonietta Barocco*. I was only in the *corps de ballet*, but it was so exhilarating to perform. I was doing well at the school and had been put in what was considered to be the best class, with students from the Royal Ballet Junior School.

After I left school I went into the *corps de ballet* of the Royal Ballet for two years. After the fully organized school days I seemed to have much more time on my hands. This was the time when I had to learn some self-discipline. I had no teacher telling me to go to class and I also had to learn how to get more out of a class myself.

My average day starts at about 8am in my flat in Ealing. I have a simple breakfast – toast, boiled eggs and muesli – while I listen to the radio or watch breakfast television. Then I drive to the studio at Baron's Court, getting there at around 10am. Most days I do a whole class, the *barre* and the centre work, but you can leave after the *barre* if you have a heavy rehearsal day. I've always liked the centre work best from my earliest days in Hong Kong. I enjoy the free movement, the expression and the *ports de bras*. I don't find all the steps equally easy. My *frappés* worry me sometimes as I have difficulty keeping the right turn-out, and sometimes I envy someone else's *arabesque,* but whatever I do, I keep trying to do better each time.

During the class I enjoy watching dancers I admire, like Merle Park, Antoinette Sibley, Alessandra Ferri, Fiona Chadwick and Bryony Brind. You can learn so much by just

watching. When Mikhail Baryshnikov and Natalia Makarova did some guest performances with us it was marvellous to work next to them in class, and students of the school would also watch through the windows in the studio doors. There isn't any personal rivalry in class as we are really all so different in our personalities and the way we dance. It's not like a sport to see who can jump highest or spin fastest. We are all, as individuals, trying to do the best we can achieve.

After the class, which lasts about an hour and a quarter, we have a short break, then the main rehearsal of the day until lunch break at 2pm. I keep off fatty things and cakes and biscuits. Nothing stodgy, either, as it is so uncomfortable to dance with a full stomach.

Rehearsals are all different depending on the sort of ballet you are working on. You are usually in a studio with the pianist, the Notator, who has the steps written down in a big book like a music score, and the choreographer or ballet master. And the rest of the cast, of course.

If you are working on one of the big classics like *Swan Lake* there can be a lot of waiting about for the *corps de ballet*, but the atmosphere is relaxed. But rehearsing solo roles in these classics is really hard work. They look so elegant and easy on stage compared to some modern ballets, though it can take hours of rehearsals to get the right speed and sharpness in a solo like that of the Finger Fairy in *The Sleeping Beauty*. I haven't yet tried the much more difficult Rose Adage in the same ballet, when Princess Aurora has to balance a long time *en attitude* to be turned around by each of her four suitors. I'd love to try it, though, as I like dancing the classics especially with the marvellous Tchaikovsky music. I love fairy tales, anyway.

Working on a new ballet with someone like Sir Frederick Ashton is very different. He is 80 now and sometimes it's just a *little* bit difficult to catch exactly what he wants and

then remember it. But his ballets are such a pleasure to dance on stage. Kenneth MacMillan's ballet, like *Manon* are different. You have to get into a difficult character part as well as do the dancing.

I have also been working in another completely different style with Arlette van Boven of Nederlands Dans Theater. She has been putting on Jiri Killian's *Return to the Strange Land* for us. It's full of fast steps and complicated lifts and spins.

After rehearsal I sometimes like to watch videos of the ballet to remind myself of the steps or make notes of any complicated counts, to help with difficult rhythms.

A full day of rehearsal can be very exhausting. I have to change my leotard several times to feel fresh. I go through a lot of shoes as well. The company allow me ten pairs a month, but if I am performing in a lot of ballets I can get through four pairs a week!

Apart from rehearsal I might have to make time for a costume fitting for some new ballet that is coming up. This is very necessary but it can be tiring standing around while costumes are pinned and unpinned or even painted. If you have a leading role in the ballet you might also have to find time to give interviews, but this hasn't happened much to me, yet.

If I am doing a performance the rehearsal will end at 4pm and I'll drive up to the Opera House in Covent Garden. Then, at about 6pm, I start getting ready. I put on my make-up, do my hair, sort out my costume and clean my shoes. I use surgical spirit on them and then put on some white pancake which leaves them looking pale pink to blend with my tights. This gives a nicer line.

By the time of Beginners call at 7.25pm, I am on stage doing some warm-up steps or practising something with my partner. All around us the stagehands will be setting the scenery and lights.

Backstage is hectic during the show and during the intervals as well, especially if there are lots of costume changes. In some theatres, for *Swan Lake*, a few of the Peasant Girls from Act One have to do a complete change in the wings to become the Swans of Act Two. If it's a very quick change there are always helping hands to assist with the hooks and eyes and zips and buttons, which is very useful if you have to change your hairstyle as well.

At the end of the performance there are the curtain calls. It was lovely to feel the shower of daffodils on Bryony Brind, Fiona Chadwick and myself after *La Bayadere*. I feel pleased to get even a couple of calls and I've never stood there wishing they would stop so that I could get home quicker. I still feel just the same excitement performing as I did when I danced *Swan Lake* at eleven. I'm just more nervous now, that's all.

Then I quickly take my make-up off, have a shower and drive home. After the drive the exhaustion usually hits me and sometimes I only have enough energy left to put my flowers in water and get myself some soup.

To make up for these long hours we do have Sundays off and a five-week summer holiday. Dancing seems to take up so much time; more than an ordinary job. You spend so much time in studios and theatres that the company almost becomes your family. I like to go to plays, films, concerts and exhibitions when I can, and I like cooking at home. I just don't seem to get much chance, though. Sunday is always free, so I do nothing much just like everyone else. I sleep late, read the papers, wash my hair, clean the flat or sew ribbons on my shoes for the next week.

I'm only just starting a career and there are lots of roles I want to dance. I know that dancers do not have long careers, many stop at thirty-five, so I'd like to do as much as I can as soon as possible.

YOUR BALLET CLASS

As a young girl, Margot Fonteyn one day saw a poster of a ballerina and asked her mother who it was. 'That's Pavlova, the greatest dancer in the world', her mother told her. 'Then I will be the second greatest', she replied. All dancers need this confidence, though they may not all grow up to be a Prima Ballerina Assoluta and President of the Royal Academy of Dancing! Nevertheless, even though they may know they will never make it to the top many dancers feel they have achieved their life's ambition through dancing. Ballet is exhausting and time-consuming, but also exciting and creative and

many become totally dedicated to their profession. It is a whole world of its own.

The professional dancer's life needs a lot of self discipline, so it is important that you learn to be independent early on. For example, try to look after your own practice clothes yourself, and make sure that they are clean and in good repair – don't leave them for someone else to deal with. Give yourself a brief moment to relax and put yourself in the right frame of mind before you begin class. Doing these things for yourself will help you to feel more confident and self-assured.

Once class has started, listen carefully and try to keep your mind on what you are being asked to do. When you first begin ballet you may find this difficult, as many of the seemingly simple movements need to be repeated very often to get them right. A good teacher will know how to keep your interest, occasionally re-arranging your syllabus steps and allowing you to relax and have fun for a while. Your teacher is there to guide and assist you through difficult moments, but there are many ways in which you can help yourself in this respect. For instance, don't be tempted to chat to your neighbour, for that means you are not listening to your teacher and are also disturbing someone else's concentration. Your teacher will correct your movements from time to time. Try to understand why and work hard to get them right. Pay attention to other pupils' corrections; they may apply to you, too!

There is no better way of learning to dance than studying with other people who are equally interested and motivated to succeed. Learning in this way, you can judge your own progress and can compare yourself to others. If you have a particular fault which needs correcting, your teacher may think it is a good idea to have private lessons. On the whole, though, learning in class is better, as private lessons tend to

concentrate on what has not been achieved rather than on what has – in other words, your bad points rather than your good points, which may make you feel rather pessimistic about your chances of succeeding. Although it requires tremendous effort, your ballet class should also be *fun* and something to be looked forward to. How much you enjoy it can be greatly helped by interesting accompanying music. Listen to the music, for it will affect how you express yourself in movement. After all, dance is an art.

Sometimes, you may feel that you are not progressing quickly enough, but be patient and trust your teacher. Years of experience will have taught him or her to look at your development and to decide on the right pace for you. Doing

too much too early can be more damaging than being held back a little.

A little discomfort is to be expected in a ballet class, but do not push yourself too hard for, however carefully you are taught, accidents can happen. If you are in real pain, tell your teacher at once and act on his or her advice.

Working in a disciplined way will not only help you to achieve much in your dancing; it should also assist you in other areas of study – and generally prepare you for life in the future. Ask any professional dancer and he or she will tell you that good concentration and a sense of self discipline are absolutely essential if you are intending to take up dancing seriously. Nevertheless, have fun!

Jennifer Penney and Mark Silver dancing as Odette and Prince Seigfreid in a performance of Swan Lake by The Royal Ballet.

SELECTED EXERCISES FROM THE GRADES

The intention of this part of the book is to show the progression through the Royal Academy of Dancing's Grades for children. It is not a teaching manual and therefore only certain steps and movements have been selected, either because their progression is obvious or because they are well-known and can be identified in the current ballet repertoire. Each grade is written with the assumption that the reader has studied the previous grades, so that where a step or movement occurs again only the points relevant to that grade are mentioned to avoid too much repetition. It also presupposes that the reader will browse through this part of the book while learning new steps with the teacher, to act as a reminder. Learning only from a book would be dull and dancing should be fun.

Alain Dubreuil and Margaret Barbieri in Façade (SWRB).

SELECTED EXERCISES FROM THE GRADES

The following exercises are part of the RAD method for both boys and girls. Apart from the first two levels all the movements in ballet are given a French name, since French is the language used for dance throughout the world.

The French names are explained when they first appear, and in a glossary at the back of the book.

Before you begin to look through the exercises and steps described in this chapter, you must first understand the five positions of the arms and feet.

The Positions of the Arms

Bras Bas

The position of the arms from which all other positions start is called *bras bas*. In English it means 'arms down' and it also serves as a resting place in between exercises. The arms, which are held a little in front of the body, should be relaxed and a little rounded at the elbow, with the fingers continuing the curve in the arm to create an oval shape. The little finger is the closest to the leg.

From *bras bas* the five basic positions of the arms can be made.

REMEMBER
○ Relax your shoulders.
○ Keep your thumbs close to the other fingers.
○ Try not to show the backs of your hands.

1st Position

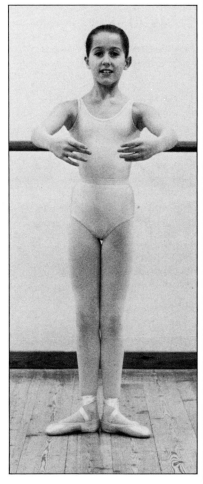

2nd Position

This is the gateway to all the other positions. You must always go through 1st position to get to any other position of the arms.

REMEMBER
○ Relax your shoulders.
○ Support your elbows.
○ Keep the palms of your hands facing you.

In this position there should be a slight slope downwards from your shoulders to your wrists —just enough to allow a small drop of water to trickle slowly down your arms.

REMEMBER
○ Keep your shoulders relaxed.
○ Keep your arms gently curved with the centre of your palms facing the front.
○ Support your elbows.

3rd Position

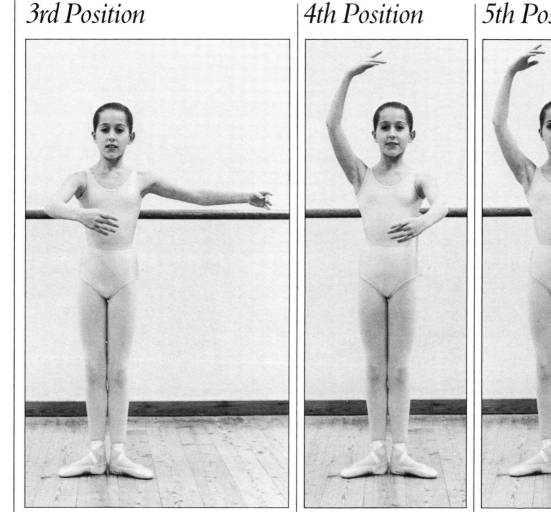

4th Position

5th Position

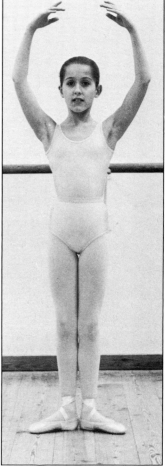

One arm is placed in 1st position and the other in 2nd position.

REMEMBER
○ Not to over-cross the arm in front.
○ All the points made regarding 1st and 2nd positions.

One arm is placed in 1st position and the other is raised high, slightly in front of the head.

REMEMBER
○ Those shoulders!
○ Check your posture—has it sagged anywhere?

Both arms are raised high with the hands a little in front of the body.

REMEMBER
○ Keep your shoulders relaxed — they will be tempted to lift with your arms.
○ Keep your palms towards you, not the audience.

In addition to these basic positions there are two more which are useful for beginning or finishing exercises.

The first is *demi-seconde*, which means 'half-second', and you will find it half-way between 2nd position and *bras bas*. The arms are held a little in front of the body.

The second is *demi-bras*, which means 'half-arms', and it is half-way between 1st and 2nd positions. In this position the hands open with the palms slightly upward as if you were asking for something (applause perhaps?). The arms are held lower than in 2nd position.

Demi-seconde

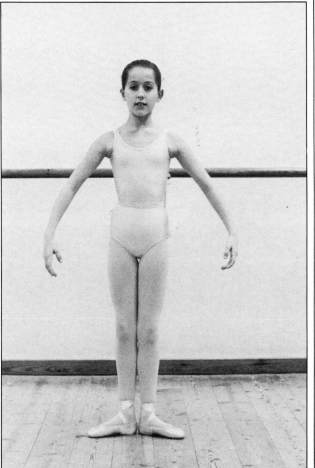

Demi-bras

Ports de Bras

When the arms move continuously through some or all of these positions it is called *ports de bras*. This actually means 'carriage of the arms', but to you it should suggest the way in which you move your arms gracefully and expressively, in harmony with the rest of your body, when you are dancing. You will find *ports de bras* exercises in each grade. They are specially designed to practise moving your arms through the different positions, and include the use of the body in later grades.

The Positions of the Feet

The amount that you can turn your feet sideways in any position will depend on how much you can make your thigh turn outwards in the hip joint so that your knee is facing the same way as your foot. (The hip joint is where your leg is joined to your body.) Never push your foot out beyond the knee as this is cheating and it will cause problems later on.

1st Position

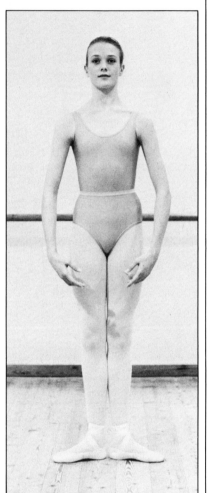

The heels are placed together with toes pointed outwards and away from each other.

2nd Position

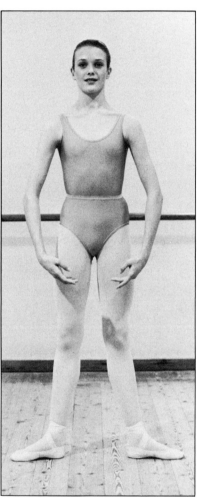

The distance between your feet should be approximately one-and-a-half times the length of your foot. Your teacher will help you to find the right position.

3rd Position

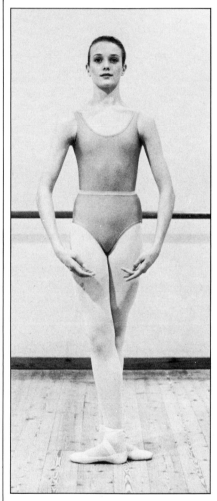

The heel of one foot is placed against the instep of the other.

4th Position

5th Position

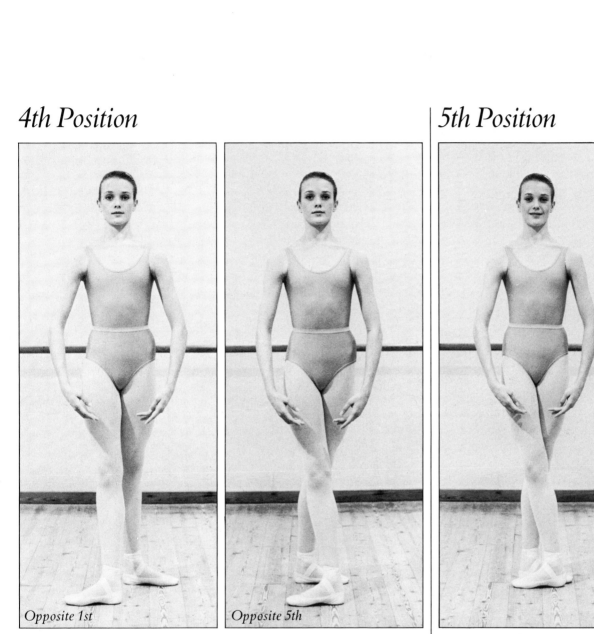

Opposite 1st

Opposite 5th

One leg is taken forward and the heels are placed opposite each other (that is, opposite 1st position).

The distance between your feet is measured as for 2nd position.

One leg is taken forward and the heel of the front foot is placed opposite the toes of the back foot (that is, opposite 5th position). The weight is placed evenly between the feet.

The distance between your feet is about the length of only one of your feet.

The heel of one foot is placed beside the toe of the other. Your amount of turnout will depend, as always, upon what you can manage, but remember — it can be improved with practice!

Good Posture

Finally, before you read further, a dancer must always think about the way he or she is standing, for *nothing* will work correctly unless the body is held upright with the weight over the feet and without any sagging or arching in the spine (the bony column that runs up and down the back, on top of which the head is poised). It takes a long time to achieve this correct posture and so, although it will not always be mentioned in each exercise, you must think about it all the time during class or when you are practising alone.

Correct posture

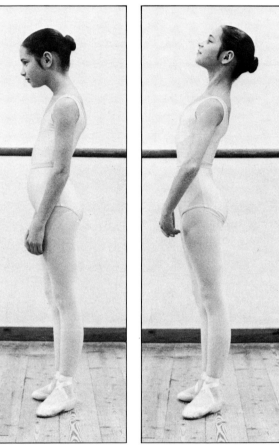

Incorrect posture:
a sagging back

Incorrect posture:
arching the back

❧ PRE-PRIMARY GRADE ❧

*At this stage you will learn to dance in many different ways,
sometimes with a partner and sometimes on your own. It should
be fun to do!*

Walking with Stretched Toes

This is an exercise from the part of the class where you do movements in a circle. All dancers must learn how to walk with stretched toes. It makes their movements look much more light and delicate. Walk round the room putting your toes on the floor first instead of your heels. See if you can find an exercise further on that will help your toes to stretch more.

Walk round the room placing the toes on the floor first. Remember to keep the back and head well lifted and listen carefully to the music.

Good Toes, Naughty Toes

This is one of the exercises that you do sitting on the floor. Sit with a very straight back and with your legs stretched out in front. Place your hands on your thighs. Now turn your feet up so that your toes are pointing to the ceiling. Your teacher may call this position 'naughty toes' since it does not look at all like a dancer's feet. Then stretch your feet fully so that they are pointing in the same direction as your legs. These are 'good toes'. Keep your legs stretched all the way up.

With a very straight back, turn your toes up to the ceiling. Now point them forwards keeping the legs stretched.

Naughty toes

Good toes

25

Knee Bends – Demi-pliés

This exercise, and the next one, are both taken from the section of the class called Technical Exercises.

Your teacher may call Knee Bends by their French name, *demi-pliés*, which actually means 'half-bends'.

Stand with your heels touching, toes slightly apart and with your body looking very straight and tall. Girls could hold the edges of their skirts out slightly if they are wearing one — it will help them to keep their balance and give the arms something to do. Boys should keep their arms in the *bras bas* position shown on page 16. Bend your knees, opening them out over your toes as if you were opening a window on either side. Is there a big space and is your back still straight and tall? Now stretch up slowly, closing your knees tightly so that there is no space left between them. Try doing this movement eight times so that you begin to get used to it. See if you can find it somewhere else in this chapter. It may be called by its French name!

Try not to lift your heels off the floor when you bend your knees.

Three Points and Close

Start as you did for Knee Bends, with your heels touching and your toes apart. This is called 1st position of the feet because it is the first and the easiest for you to learn. Have you got very tight knees to help you balance? If so, slide one leg forward until you have made 'good toes'. Keeping your foot like that, tap your toes on the ground three times and then close that foot to the other one. Now try with the other leg. Do it all again — it will be useful when you get to Primary Grade.

Stretch one leg and foot forwards and lightly tap the ground three times with your toes. Then slide it back again. Try with the other leg. Keep the back and head well lifted to help you balance.

Bounces

Bounces come in the part of the class called Free Movement, where you do things such as running and pretending to be dolls, fairies, cats, clowns or birds. For Bounces, your feet are side by side. Bounce up and down as high as you can like a big rubber ball—the Knee Bends you have practised will come in useful. Stretch your toes in the air, and do not forget to bend your knees for a soft landing. Can you do 16 all in one go?

Keeping your feet side by side, bounce up and down like a rubber ball. The more you stretch your legs and feet the higher you will go. Try to bounce in time with the music.

Galops

Towards the end of your class you will do some dance steps, which include trotting, galoping, and joining simple steps together.

Galoping is fun because it is done with a partner from one corner of the room across to the other, in a long diagonal line.
Start with your feet together, facing and holding your partner. Step sideways (with your toes going down first if you are clever!) and then spring your feet together in the air as you did in the bouncing exercise. Come down on one foot, with the other ready to step to the same side again. Keep doing this until you have reached the other corner. Can you find this step in another grade?

Hold your partner tightly and remember to make the galops bounce!

Révérence

At the end of the class your teacher will show you how to thank her, and the pianist if one has come to play for you. It will be with either a curtsey or a bow, depending on whether you are a girl or a boy.

Curtsey (girls)

Raise one arm forward towards the person you are thanking and place one foot behind the other, making a good firm platform with the toes. Slowly bend the knee that you are standing on, – trying not to wobble (keeping the back straight will help) and then slowly straighten up again. Try with the other foot and arm now. Your teacher may like you to do a step to the side before the curtsey.

Bow (boys)

Looking at the person you are thanking, stand very proudly in 1st position with your arms hanging by your side. Slowly lower the eyes, letting the head drop forwards a little. Take the same amount of time to lift it up again. Try again. Your teacher may want you to step to the side first, before bowing the head.

Curtsey

Bow

'Come on it's our turn now!'

Demi-Plié

Do you remember Knee Bends from Pre-Primary? You learned then that *demi-pliés*, their French name, means 'half-bends', and in this grade they are done with your feet in 1st position only. There are two counts for bending your knees and two to straighten your knees carefully and tightly. The movement will make the muscles in your legs stretch gently while you keep your balance over your feet. *Demi-plié* is very useful and important because all springing steps begin and end with it. You will come across it often from now on.

REMEMBER
○ Keep your knees out over your toes.
○ Keep your back straight.
○ Don't look down to see if you have got it right!

The knees bend with the body placed in the centre of the feet and without raising the heels. The knees are placed over the toes, with the back held upright and the head poised.

Walk and Point

Do you remember Walking with Stretched Feet and Three Points from Pre-Primary? In this grade you are going to put the two together. To make it a little harder, after three walks forward there will only be one point forward and the leg you are standing on will be bent. This is done in a circle so that you can keep practising it. When you can do it well, your teacher may allow you to use your arms, too.

REMEMBER
○ Keep your head well poised, as if you were wearing a crown.
○ Keep your back up to match your head.
○ Don't turn the foot of your bent leg out so far that your knee cannot catch up with it!

Place your bent knee over your toes and try to turn your stretched leg out so that its knee is pointing away from the bent one. Hold your back still.

Point Lift, Point Close

This will eventually become a movement called *grand battement*. In this grade it is taken in four movements, and it is to test how you place your leg in front of you and whether you can lift it off the ground and balance there without wobbling. It starts in 1st position and your arms are held out at the sides to help you to balance.

REMEMBER
○ Pull your tummy up to help your back stay upright.
○ Keep the knee of the leg you are standing on tight.
○ Don't look to see if it is!
○ Try to make it look easy. This will be difficult until you have practised it over and over again.

1 Starting position for the Point Lift and Point Close exercise.

2 Stretch out your leg in front of you, just like you did in the Pre-Primary exercise for your feet. Then lift it just two or three inches off the floor.

3 Pull your tummy up tightly to hold your leg still and keep the leg you are standing on very straight to help you to balance. Lower your leg slowly so that you do not bang your foot on the floor, then close in 1st position.

Ports de Bras

Do you remember what this means? In Pre-Primary you learned to use your arms in a rather free way. Now you are going to move them from one position to another, learning to make a good shape in each and keeping them soft and flowing. If you use your head and eyes as well it will look even nicer.

Galops

In this grade, *galops* travel forwards as well as sideways. Even though you are learning to place them more carefully and to add the use of arms, if you are clever enough they should still be a light bouncy movement. Remember to start the first *galop* with a hop to get you going. When you take the *galop* sideways, your feet should join side by side in the air, like 1st position of the feet.

1 Hop with the leading leg and foot stretched out in front and then step on to it.

2 Close your back foot to your front foot with a spring in the air, toes well pointed.

1
Travelling forwards

2

1
Travelling sideways

2

REMEMBER
○ Bounce!
○ Keep your back and arms still as you travel.

Bryony Brind in the studio – even professional dancers have to practise daily.

Exercise for Head Movement

This is an exercise for the part that your head plays in turning steps. You will find that it stops you from getting dizzy when you start to turn in the later grades. (Try to find out where that is!)

4 Recover with your body facing square to the front, your eyes still fixed on your spot. Try it again, but the other way round this time.

3 When you can no longer keep your eyes on your spot, whip your head to the other side and find your spot again, bringing your body round gradually to the front.

2 Shifting your feet a little at a time on the same spot, begin to turn your body away from the front, keeping your eyes fixed on your spot.

1 Place your hands lightly on your shoulders and find something in front of you upon which to fix your eyes.

REMEMBER
○ Don't tilt your body as you turn away from the front or you might lose your balance.
○ Keep your head straight as you whip it from one side to the other.
○ Don't lose your spot!

Monica Mason in the role of Chosen Maiden, created for her by Kenneth MacMillan in his version of Rite of Spring, first performed by The Royal Ballet at Covent Garden in 1962.

Sautés

A *sauté* is a spring and it begins and ends in a *demi-plié*. Instead of just bouncing like you did in Pre-Primary, you are going to learn how to stretch your feet fully in the air and how to come down with your heels together, your knees open and back held upright — all without a noise. If this sounds difficult, it is!

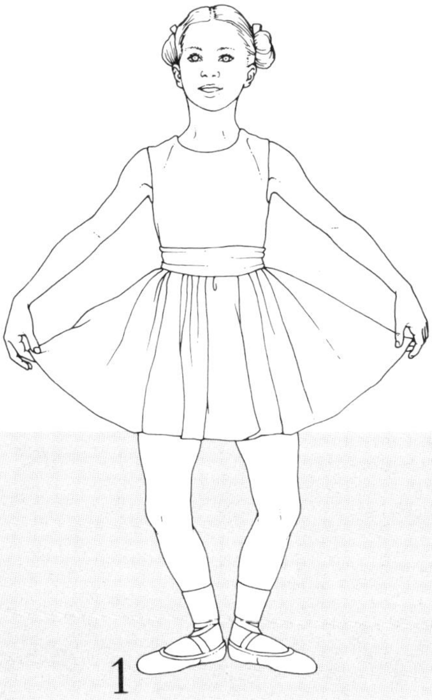

REMEMBER
○ Stretch your legs and feet well in the air, otherwise you will be in danger of looking like a frog!
○ Land quietly, toes first then heels, with your back well lifted and your knees *open*.

1 Make a *demi-plié*.

Echappés Sautés

Echappér means 'to escape' and this is an 'escaping' movement. The step begins like the *sautés* in 1st position that you have already learned, but at the top of the spring in the air, your feet 'escape' from each other and arrive on the ground in 2nd position. Only boys do this step in Primary, because much of their dancing contains springing steps and they must learn how to push themselves into the air as soon as possible. However, there is nothing to stop girls from having a go!

REMEMBER
○ Stretch your feet and legs well to push yourself into the air.
○ Keep your back upright, particularly when you come down into *demi-plié*.
○ That it is difficult!

1

2

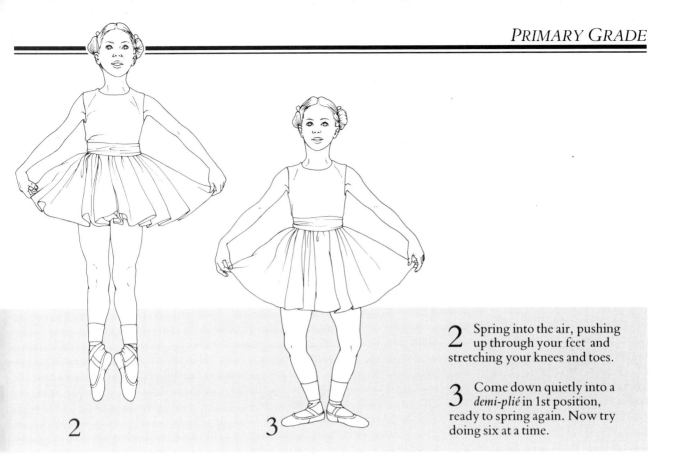

2 Spring into the air, pushing up through your feet and stretching your knees and toes.

3 Come down quietly into a *demi-plié* in 1st position, ready to spring again. Now try doing six at a time.

1 Start in *demi-plié*.

2 Spring into the air, keeping your feet close together.

3 Open your feet in the air and come down in *demi-plié*, 2nd position — not *too* wide.

4 Spring into the air from 2nd position, stretching your feet well.

5 Come down in a *demi-plié* in 1st position. After several springs, finish calmly with your feet in 1st position and arms in *bras bas*.

Révérence

This is the traditional way in which a dancer thanks the teacher for his or her care and encouragement, and the pianist for the music that he or she has provided for the class.

Once the curtsey and bow have been described here they will not be referred to again because they will stay the same all the way through the grades — but do not forget to practise them.

Curtsey (girls)

1 Start with your feet in 1st position.

2 Step to the side and open your arm, with the palm slightly upwards, towards the person you are thanking.

3 Close your other foot behind the leg you are standing on, with your toes on the floor and your heel lifted. Bend the supporting leg, lowering your eyes a little at the same time and keeping your arm where it is. Stretch your knee and repeat the movement to the other side, opening your arm towards the next person to be thanked.

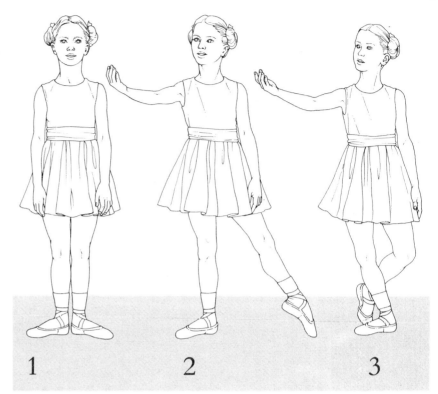

Bow (boys)

1 Start with your feet in 1st position.

2 Step sideways, opening your arm, with the palm slightly upwards, towards the person to be thanked.

3 Close your foot in 1st position, with no weight on it. Bow your head and shoulders forward a little. Recover to an upright position and step the other way, raising the other arm to repeat the movement to the other side.

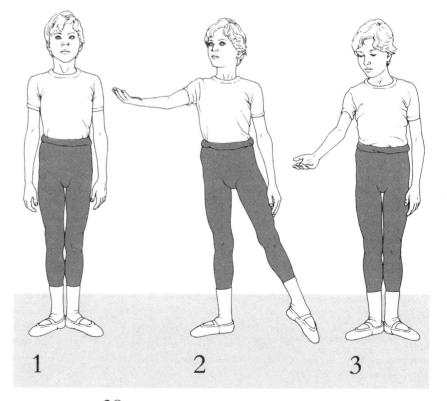

☙ GRADE ONE ☙

Now that you have reached this standard, you will begin to work through the class like a professional dancer. From now on, the exercises are divided into two parts—those taken at the barre, and those in the centre.

AT THE BARRE

This is where the dancer stands with either one or two hands lightly resting on a supported bar of wood (or perhaps the back of a chair in your school) which is approximately the same height as your hip. It is here that you will learn to do your basic movements correctly and gain more control while being gently supported. Your body should always be held well, with your weight over your feet. On no account should you lean on or pull away from the *barre*.

Demi-Plié

This will now also be taken in 2nd and 3rd positions of the feet. With a *barre* to hold you should be more successful in keeping your knees sideways over your toes during the bending movement, your back kept upright and your head well poised.

1 With feet in 2nd position, bend the knees a little (your teacher will tell you how low to go) pressing them out sideways as you lower until they are sitting over your toes.

2 With the feet in 3rd position, bend the knees, pressing them out to the side as before, until you can go no further without raising the heels from the ground.

Battements Tendus

Battement means 'beating' and *tendu* means 'stretched'. This exercise is to help lengthen your leg muscles and strengthen the insteps of your feet. In this grade it is taken from 1st position to the side (*à la seconde*) facing the *barre*, and to the front (*devant*) and the back (*derrière*) sideways with one hand on the *barre*. Where have you come across a simple version of the one to the front before?

In Grade One this movement is rather quick to the side. Practise it slowly so that you have time to remember everything.

Because this is such an important movement you will find it in every grade and in every professional dancers' class.

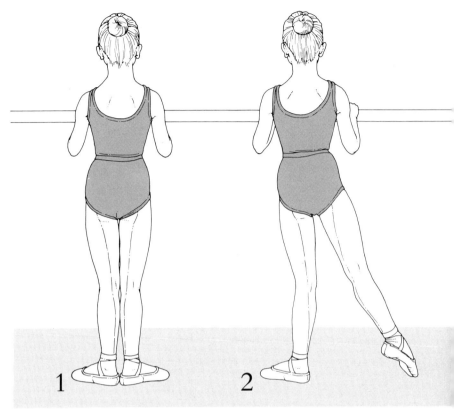

Battement Tendu devant

1 Start in 1st position with your legs and feet evenly turned out to the side. Place your free arm in 2nd position. The arm holding the *barre* should be relaxed and a little in front of your body.

2 Slide your foot forwards in the same manner as that described for 2nd position, keeping the heel of your working foot opposite 1st position. When it has arrived be sure that your leg is fully stretched and evenly turned out. Draw your foot gradually back to 1st position as before and check that you are as tall and upright as you were when you began.

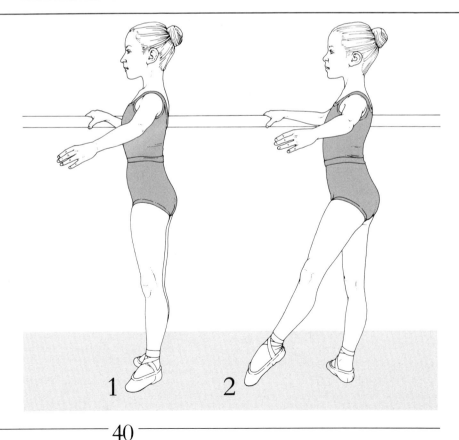

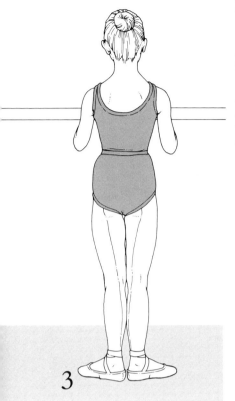

3

Battement Tendu à la seconde

1 Stand facing the *barre* with your feet opened out evenly in 1st position. Your hands should be no further apart than your shoulders.

2 Slide one foot slowly out to the side, keeping your weight over your supporting leg (the one you are standing on) and your toes on the ground until your foot is fully stretched. Your heel should show reluctance to come off the floor so that you can use plenty of pressure through your foot. Keep the inside edge of your heel facing the *barre* throughout its journey.

3 To bring your foot back to 1st position, draw it in towards you, first relaxing your toes, then your instep and then placing your heel to the ground, gradually sliding it back to 1st position. Does that leg match the other in the amount that it is turned out? Now try it all again with the other leg.

REMEMBER
○ Keep your working leg as evenly turned out as the one you are standing on.
○ Try not to do this by allowing your hips to turn away from the *barre*. That is cheating!
○ Take care not to turn your feet out further than your knees.
○ Try to stay as tall as you were at the beginning when you start to slide your leg out. Don't 'sit' on top of the other leg.

Battement Tendu derrière

Slide your foot out behind your body as before until your leg is fully stretched, with the working heel opposite the supporting heel and your toe resting gently on the floor. This is the most difficult of the *tendus* to make because you cannot see it and therefore you cannot be sure that you have succeeded. Your teacher will help you to feel when it is in the right place. Draw your foot back to 1st position as before, making sure that the underneath of your foot is touching the floor when it arrives back to 1st position.

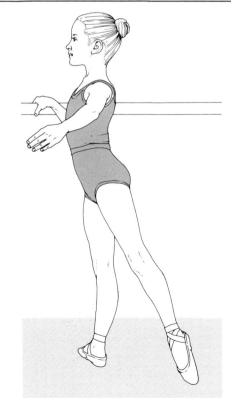

REMEMBER
○ Arrive back in 1st position with your feet looking equal.

Grands Battements

Grand means 'big' or 'large'. This movement will eventually be like throwing the leg high into the air, although the throwing action does not happen until Grade Three, where it will loosen your leg at the hip joint (do you remember how to find that?) and eventually help you to lift your foot high above your waistline. Until then you will be learning how to place your body and leg only. In Grade One the movement is divided into four and is taken only *devant* and *derrière* from 1st position.

1   2

Grands Battements derrière
(facing the *barre*)

1   Start in 1st position, facing the *barre*.

2   Stretch one leg out *derrière*.

3   Carefully lift your leg a little off the ground, keeping your back and both legs straight.

4   Lower your foot to the floor. Close your foot to 1st position, making sure that it is as turned out as the other one when it arrives.

1   2

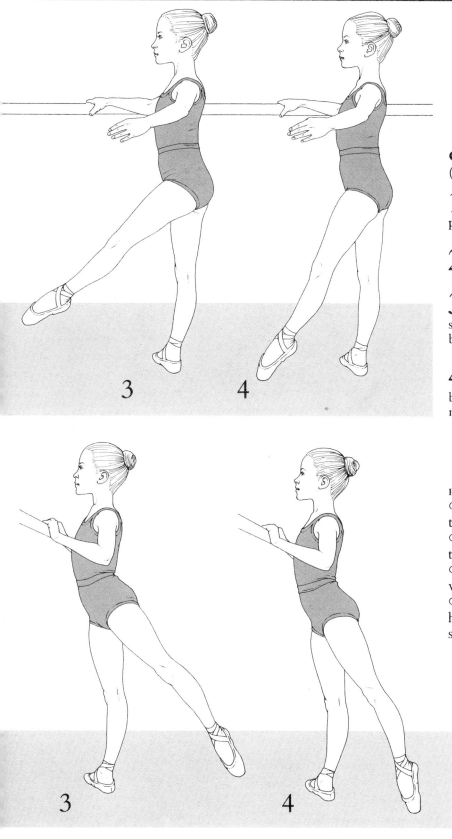

Grands Battements devant
(sideways to *barre*)

1 Stand in 1st position with your free arm in 2nd position.

2 Point the leg that is furthest away from the *barre devant*.

3 Lift your leg into the air without bending the supporting knee or letting your back go.

4 Lower your foot to the floor. Close your foot carefully back to 1st position so that it matches the other.

REMEMBER
○ Keep your back well lifted throughout.
○ Keep your legs stretched throughout.
○ Keep *both* hips facing the barre when taking your leg *derrière*.
○ Listen to the music — it will help you to make the movement strong.

Preparation for Pirouette

A *pirouette* is a turn or spin on one leg. In this grade you are going to learn where to place your other leg when turning, so that you will be ready to have a try in the centre later on. The preparation is taken facing the *barre* for better balance.

Girls

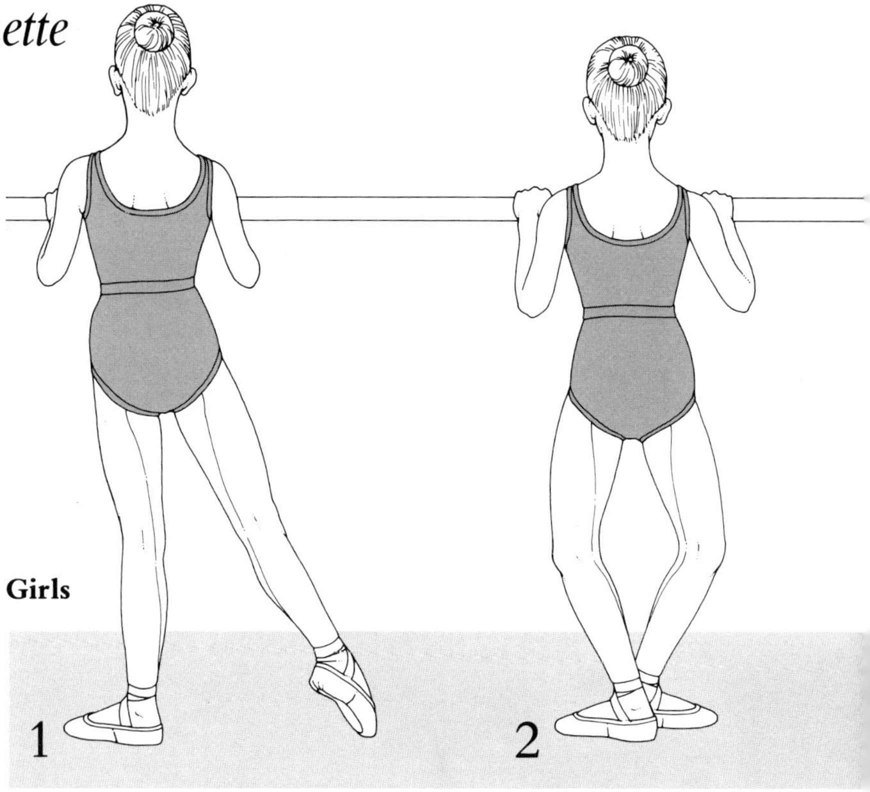

1

2

Boys
The boys make their *demi-plié* in 2nd position before lifting one foot under the knee.

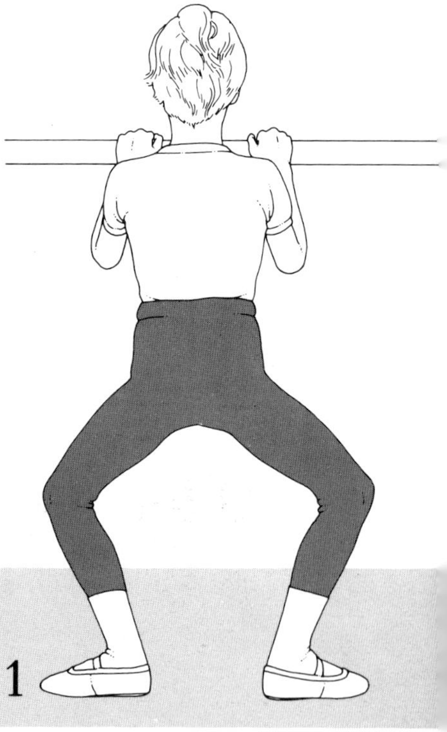

1

REMEMBER
○ Keep your knees turned out in the *demi-plié* in 2nd position.
○ Stand right over the leg when making the *pirouette* position.

3

1   Start in 1st position. Stretch your right foot to the side (like a *battement tendu*).

2   Draw your foot back to 3rd position and lower into *demi-plié*, keeping your back straight and well lifted.

3   Stretch your left leg firmly, placing your right foot quickly under your knee in *pirouette* position★. Close your right foot back to 1st position. Then try it all again with the other leg.

1   Start in 1st position. Stretch your right foot to the side (like a *battement tendu*). Lower the foot into *demi-plié* in second position.

2   Stretch your left leg firmly, placing your right foot quickly under your knee in *pirouette* position. Close your right foot back to 1st position. Then try it all again with the other leg.

IN THE CENTRE

This is where the dancer practises movements without the help of the *barre*. Some of the steps travel and some stay in one place.

Ports de Bras

In this grade, *ports de bras* includes 5th position of the arms as well as those used in Primary Grade. Practise the movement from 5th position to 2nd position so that you can do it without any stiffness in the arms.

Battements Tendus en face

En face means 'facing the front' (see Directions of the Body, page 56). This exercise is made up of two of the *battements tendus* from the *barre* put together to test your balance when taking one foot away from the other. You will find the movement faster in the centre. Listen carefully to the music.

REMEMBER
○ Keep your body still and well lifted.
○ Keep your legs well stretched, particularly the one on which you are standing.
○ Make your movements smooth and controlled.

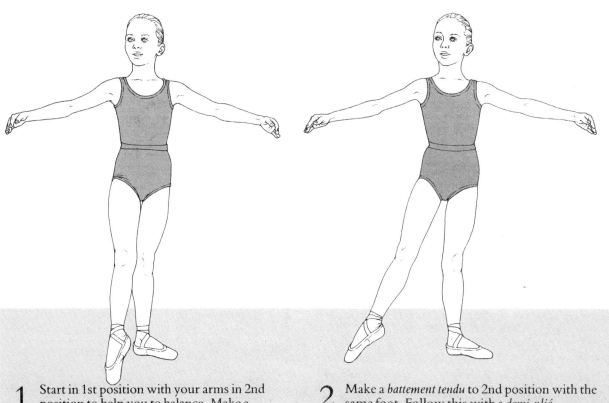

1 Start in 1st position with your arms in 2nd position to help you to balance. Make a *battement tendu devant* with the right foot closing back to 1st position.

2 Make a *battement tendu* to 2nd position with the same foot. Follow this with a *demi-plié*, bringing your arms to *bras bas* to give everything a rest before you repeat it with the other leg.

Galops and Pas de Cheval

The *galops* have already been practised on their own. Here they will still travel forwards but with another step added, *pas de cheval*. This means 'step of the horse', because it looks a little like a horse braying and pawing the ground.

Pas de Cheval

Practise this movement on its own, making sure that the downward and upward movements are firm and that each takes an equal amount of time. Then practise the whole movement round the room, using the *pas de cheval* foot to start another set of *galops*.

REMEMBER
○ Stand on a straight leg when you are imitating the horse.
○ Keep your foot fully pointed when 'pawing' the ground.

1 After four *galops* with your right foot, bring your back leg forwards through 1st position, fully stretched in the 4th opposite 1st position, with your other knee straight to help you balance. (Note the position of the front hand and the head.)

2 Raise your left foot sharply, lightly touching the front of your other leg with the tip of your pointed toes, and toss your head. (Note what the front arm is up to.) To repeat the movement, stretch your leg, lowering your pointed foot to the ground.

Exercise for Head Movement

This is just like the exercise in Primary Grade, but with bounces instead of shuffling the feet, to prepare you for springs that turn in the air. Do not forget to fix your eyes on one spot in front of you before beginning, and try not to lose sight of it as you turn away.

Preparation for Pirouette (Boys)

This exercise practises taking the weight of your body from two feet to one, and from open positions to closed, in preparation for a turn in Grade Three. Although designed specifically for boys, girls should try it too!

REMEMBER
○ Keep your knees back over your toes in the *demi-plié* in 2nd position.
○ Place yourself in the middle of your feet in the *demi-plié* in 2nd position.
○ In order to find your balance, push your weight all the way back over the standing leg, with none left on your pointed foot.

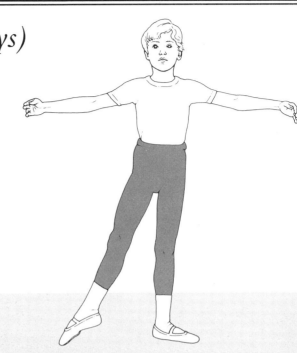

1 Start in 1st position, arms in 2nd position. Stretch your right leg firmly to 2nd position.

2 Lower carefully into a *demi-plié*, holding your back still and keeping your head and eyes steady.

3 Push firmly off your right leg until your foot is fully pointed again and your body is back over a straight left knee. Close to 1st position and then try the other leg, holding your arms in place.

Two young people obviously having fun at the end of a class, by which time even the neatest dancer can become untidy! Can you spot how many mistakes in grooming there are?

Enchaînement

This means 'linking', and is the name given to two or more steps when they are linked together and danced to several bars of music. It can contain different directions of the body, floor patterns and arm and head movements, as well as positions and movements for the legs and feet.

When all these things work in harmony with the music to produce a movement which flows from one position to another, it is called 'co-ordinated'. These *enchaînements* may be set already in the grade so that you can practise co-ordination, or they may be free (that is, given by your teacher or examiner on the spur of the moment), to see if you have an alert brain and quick reactions.

❧ GRADE TWO ❧

This grade also begins with barre work and from now on the exercises will become more complicated.

AT THE BARRE

Pliés

These will be taken in 1st, 2nd and 3rd positions, but because you will now be doing *grands*, or full, *pliés*, you will still face the *barre*, holding it with two hands to help you to do the new *pliés* well.

A *grand plié* is a full bending of your knees until your thighs are horizontal to the floor. A *grand plié* always passes through a *demi-plié*, both on the way down and on the way up, which is why you have spent so much time practising the *demi-plié* in previous grades. To begin with, let us look at the *grand plié* in 1st position.

Grand Plié in 1st Position

In this position your heels are allowed to rise gradually off the floor, but not until you have reached the depth of a *demi-plié*. The movement downwards should be very smooth, and when you have arrived in the position shown in the picture, your knees should still be over your toes, your back should still be upright and placed over your feet (rather than behind them, which makes you look as if you are going to sit down!), and you should be able to feel all of your toes on the floor.

Now comes the hard part. Having lowered yourself gracefully into the *grand plié*, you must now begin to rise up out of it with equal grace and control, lowering your heels as soon as possible — without allowing your back to sag or your knees to fall forwards — until your legs are fully stretched. It is important to remember that coming up takes just as long as going down, so that there is no jerking of the muscles — they don't like it!

REMEMBER
○ Press your knees out over your toes.
○ Keep your back straight.
○ Keep the movement smooth.
○ Don't look to see if you have got it right.

2nd Position

The *grand plié* in 2nd position is different. Because 2nd position is what we call an 'open' position rather than a 'closed' one like 1st and 3rd positions, where the feet are side by side or one just in front of the other, the full movement is taken without raising your heels. It is like a deeper *demi-plié* and you stop bending when your thighs are horizontal to the floor. It is very easy to 'sit' in this position, with your back forwards rather than upright, so be careful.

3rd Position

The *grand plié* in 3rd position is done in the same way as in 1st position but with one extra thing to remember: on the downward movement be careful not to let your heels slip away from the *barre*. If you have done it correctly you will feel your back heel pressing slightly against the front one. Don't look — just try to feel it.

Battements Glissés

Glisser means 'to slide' or 'to glide'. This is the first time that you have met a *glissé* and it will teach you how to push your leg and foot out quickly and with energy without losing control over it. There are two steps in the higher grades, *assemblés* and *jetés*, where this movement will prove useful because it will help you to spring high into the air.

In this grade the exercise is taken from 1st position only, with two hands on the *barre* to help you achieve the correct action of the leg without losing your balance. There is a *demi-plié* in the middle to allow your legs to rest a little before you try the movement on the other side. The pointing of your foot should improve if you do this exercise well.

1 Start in 1st position. With the weight of your body held firmly over your supporting leg, begin to push your foot sideways along the floor.

Battements Tendus

You have already learned the positions in which *battements tendus* may be taken in Grade One. Now they will be executed from 3rd position (not 1st) and will be done in a particular sequence: to the front, to the side and then to the back. This sequence of movements is called *en croix*, which means in the shape of a cross.

REMEMBER
○ Keep your turnout even.
○ Make the movement smooth and gradual.
○ Maintain good posture.

When stretching your leg to the front or to the back from 3rd position, notice that the position of your leg is more crossed.

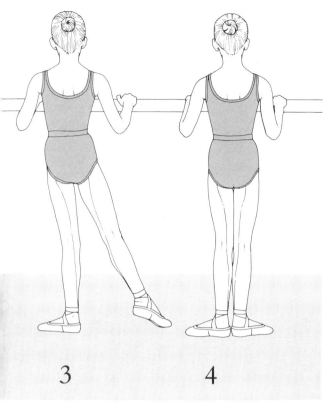

3

4

2 If you use the right amount of energy for the pushing movement, your foot should arrive in 2nd position just off the floor, beautifully stretched and evenly turned out. There are two counts for this part, one for the journey and one to hold your leg still when it has arrived.

3 Now return your leg to 1st position with the same firmness, lowering the heel of your foot as soon as possible as you draw it in.

4 Did your leg arrive home with one count left to show a good 1st position, feet evenly turned out and relaxed? Keep practising it.

REMEMBER
○ Keep your body still and square to the *barre*.
○ Don't allow your foot to come off the ground more than an inch or two. The lower it is, the more clever you have been!
○ Don't look at your foot — try to feel the right position. Your teacher will help you.

Time to relax

Grands Battements en Croix

In this grade your feet start in 3rd position. The *grand battement* is just like that in Grade One, except that it is taken in each position *en croix*, and so you will do the movement to 2nd position as well as *devant* and *derrière*. You also stand sideways to the *barre* throughout.

REMEMBER
○ Keep your hips and back still.
○ Keep your knees evenly turned out, particularly in the new 2nd position.

1 *Grand battement devant.* Start sideways to the *barre*, feet in 3rd position and arm in 2nd position.

2 *Grand battement* to 2nd position.

3 *Grand battement derrière.*

Preparation for Pirouette

This is much the same as in Grade One, but a strong rise is added into the *pirouette* position in order to find your balance and bring it much closer to the real thing. In the next grade you will be testing your balance in the centre, without the aid of a *barre*.

Girls

1 Take the preparation as for Grade One, keeping your back well lifted.

2 Then rise firmly into the *pirouette* position, supported on a strong, straight leg. Close your foot to 1st position as you lower your supporting heel.

REMEMBER
○ Keep your back straight and well lifted all the time.
○ Stand over your leg when making the *pirouette* position.

Boys

1 Take the preparation from *demi-plié* in 2nd position.

2 Boys have further to bring their weight back over their supporting leg because the preparation is taken from an open position. Be careful!

Ports de Bras

In this grade the *ports de bras* uses mainly 4th position of the arms and includes a slight turning movement in the body. Listen to the music to help you to keep your arms soft and flowing. Boys have their own special *ports de bras* in Grade Two to develop poise and style like a true *danseur noble* (a dancer of fine appearance). When you take your three walks, stride out firmly, placing your toes down *before* your heels.

Directions of the Body

Each of the different ways in which the body can face towards an audience has a special name. The direction you learned in Grade One was *en face*, which means standing yourself 'square to' or facing, the front. In this grade you will use *en croisé* and *en écarté* as well. Have a look at the drawings below and use them for further study when you move on to the other grades.

There are more directions, but these are the four that you need to know for the grades in the Children's Syllabus. Do not forget to position the head and eyes as well, for they will add the final touch. The placing of *en effacé* is shown clearly in Grade Three. Can you find it?

En face (facing)
The feet could be in any position on the ground or in the air, as long as the body faces front.

En croisé (crossed)
One side of the body is turned away from the front with the leg nearest the audience crossed in front of the other (in 3rd position for Grade Two). The front leg can be extended forwards (or the back leg to the back) on the ground (*á terre*) or in the air (*en l'air*).

En effacé
One side of your body is turned away from the front with the leg furthest away from the audience placed in front (in 3rd or 5th position for Grade Three onwards). As in *en croisé*, one leg could be stretched away from the other.

En écarté
This means 'separated' or 'thrown apart' and can be achieved by stretching one leg to 2nd position with your body turned slightly away from the audience. Your head should be looking over your front shoulder.

IN THE CENTRE

Battements Tendus — en croisé and en écarté

First of all, study the drawings on page 56 showing all the different directions of the body.
In this grade the *battements tendus* will go to all the positions that you learned at the *barre*, but will face different ways.

REMEMBER
○ Push your foot along the floor with pressure—both on the opening and closing movements.
○ Move your weight totally from one leg to the other when changing from *devant* to *derrière* to *écarté*.
○ Always keep your body strong and well lifted.

Glissade

This is a gliding step which stays close to the ground and which serves either as a preparation before big springs or as a link from one step to another. In this grade you will learn *glissade devant* and *derrière*, with three counts for each one.

Glissades derrière

Have you guessed which foot starts the *glissade derrière*? The only difference from *glissade devant*, apart from the starting foot, is that your arms are held in *bras bas* all the time—they do not move to 3rd position.

REMEMBER
○ Make good use of your legs and feet to create the lift in the middle.
○ Keep both knees turned out, particularly when closing your second leg into 3rd position.

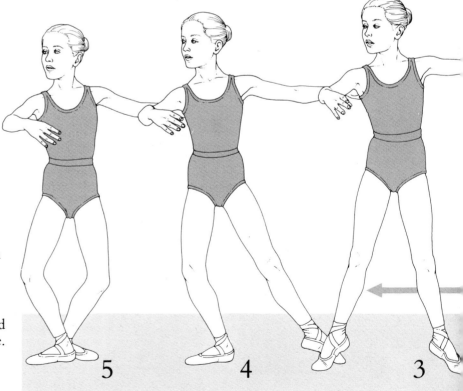

1 Start in 3rd position with your right foot front, facing the *croisé* direction, and with your arms in 'attitude in opposition' — a new position in which the arm opposite the front foot is placed high.

2 Do two *battements tendus devant* with your right leg, holding your arms still and poising your head with your eyes to the audience.

3 Keep your arms, heads and eyes as they are and do two *battements tendus derrière* with your left leg.

4 Follow this with four *battements tendus en écarté*, with your right leg, lowering your raised arm to 2nd position with the first one and looking over your front shoulder.

Lower your arms to *bras bas* and then repeat it all again to the other *croisé* direction — that is, with your left foot in front and facing the other way.

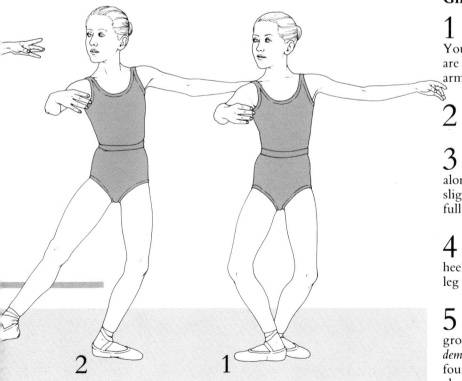

Glissades devant

1 Start in *demi-plié* with your right foot in front in 3rd position. Your arms are in *bras bas* or, if you are able, in 3rd position. The right arm is forwards.

2 Slide your right foot out to 2nd position until your knee is straight.

3 Push firmly off your left leg, sending the other a little further along the floor and lifting yourself slightly into the air until both feet are fully stretched.

4 Shift your weight over and bend your right leg, lowering your heel to the ground. Leave your left leg fully stretched.

5 Keeping your right leg bent, slide your left foot along the ground into 3rd position *derrière* in *demi-plié*. Now start it all again. Try four together, travelling sideways along the floor.

Balancé de Côté (Girls)

Balancer means 'to rock or sway', and *de côté* means 'from side to side', and therefore this is a step which rocks from side to side, with the head, body and arms swaying in unison. Listen to the music. It is a waltz and will help you to keep the rocking smooth.

REMEMBER
○ Push your knees out sideways throughout.
○ Take a large step sideways to make it move well.
○ Make the lifting movement that follows gentle.
○ Dance it!

Balancé de Côté (Boys)

The boys' version has the same footwork but is more springing and energetic and has two different arm movements to choose from.

Version One

1 Start in 3rd position, left foot front, in *demi-plié* with your hands on your hips.

2 As you spring from the left foot to the right, sweep your right arm forwards and out to the side, lifting it a little higher than 2nd position. Turn your shoulders a little with your arm but leave your head and eyes to the front.

3 With your *balancé* to the left, sweep your right arm across your body, placing your hand to a position just in front of your left shoulder. Use your shoulders and head as before. Try several more.

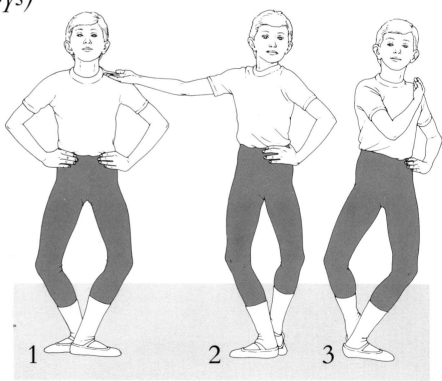

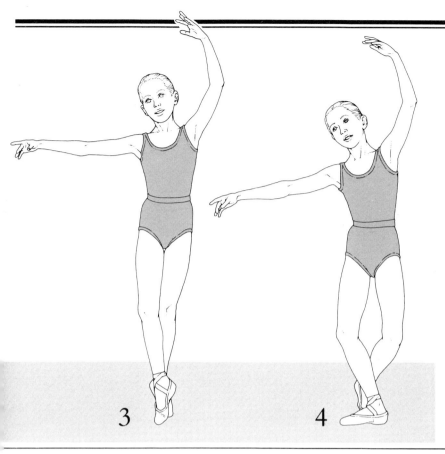

1 Starting in *demi-plié* in 3rd position, left foot front, slide your right leg out to 2nd position, arms in attitude in opposition. (Where else have you used that arm position?)

2 Push off your left leg on to the right with the same action as a *glissade*, changing your arms overhead and leaning your head and body to the right. Count: one.

3 Bring your left foot in behind your right ankle and momentarily take the weight on to the ball (or pad) of your left foot, holding your arms still and beginning to stretch the instep of the right foot. Count: two.

4 Before your right foot has time to fully stretch, lower your weight on to it again. Count: three. Do it all again the other way, leaning the head and body to the left and changing your arms overhead. Try several at a time.

Version Two

1 Start in *demi-plié* as before and with the first *balancé* to the right, release your hands from your hips and fold your arms across your body (left in front, right behind), turning your shoulders to the right and leaving your head and eyes to the front.

2 With your *balancé* left, swing your arms sideways and change them over. These arms give the step a Spanish look. Try several and then start it all to the left.

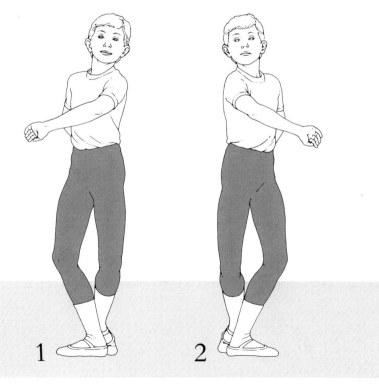

REMEMBER
○ Make a wide, low spring sideways on the rock from side to side so that it moves well.
○ Use your shoulders carefully or they may pull the second knee forwards.
○ Keep it strong — the music will help.

Petits Jetés

Petit means 'little' and *jeté* 'thrown'. This is a small version of a step which consists of springing from one foot to the other with the arms in *bras bas*.

REMEMBER
○ Use your legs and feet fully.
○ Keep your body still.
○ Breathe!
○ Bounce!

Preparation for Pirouette (Boys)

This is one stage further than Grade One and involves lifting your foot to *pirouette* position as at the *barre* and using proper arms, to test your balance further. This is a good exercise for the girls, too.

REMEMBER
○ Put your weight exactly between your feet in *demi-plié*.
○ Be careful not to push *too* hard into *pirouette* position or you might fall over!

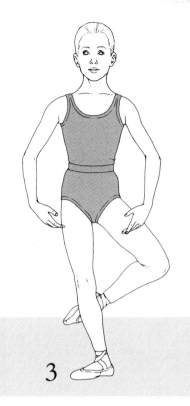

1 Look at the drawing on the far left. One foot is fully pointed with the heel placed closely behind the ankle of the other. The right knee is bent and facing sideways. The foot is said to be *sur le cou-de-pied derrière*.

2 Spring into the air by pushing off your left leg, fully stretching your knee and foot.

3 Come down softly on to your right leg with your knee bent over your toes, placing your left foot behind the plump part of your right lower leg (called the calf). Try several together — at least sixteen!

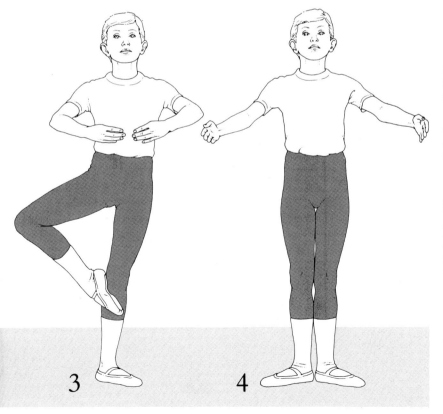

1 Start in 1st position, arms *bras bas*. Stretch the right foot firmly to 2nd position, opening the arms through 1st to arrive in 2nd position at the same time.

2 Lower carefully into *demi-plié* in 2nd position, bringing the right arm forward to make 3rd position.

3 Push up, placing the weight firmly on to your left leg and bringing your right foot to *pirouette* position. The left arm joins the right also to make *pirouette* position. (This is like a shrunken 1st position, so that the arms do not stick out too much and slow down the turn — or turns!)

4 Recover to 1st position, opening the arms to *demi-bras* to help keep you forwards over your feet. To try it to the other side, open your arms further to 2nd position as your left foot moves to the side.

Echappés Sautés

This is a step that the boys first learned in Primary. Look up the meaning and description of the step. Instead of beginning in 1st position, place your feet in 3rd position and change them over on each closing. To make it more difficult, take your arms from *bras bas* to 1st position with the spring upwards, and then into 2nd position as the feet come down in 2nd. Hold them there until you have completed two *échappés sautés* and then bring them back to *bras bas* with the closing.

When you move your arms as described above, the whole thing is called a 'simple *ports de bras*', so here you are doing one simple *ports de bras* to two *échappés sautés*.

Changements (Girls)

This means 'changing' and *changements* are springs changing the feet in the air.

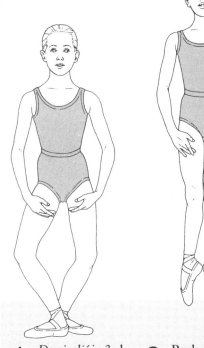

REMEMBER
○ Make them bounce.
○ Lower your heels firmly in *demi-plié*.
○ Keep your posture upright.
○ Keep your arms still — don't heave yourself into the air with them.

1 *Demi-plié* in 3rd position, right foot front, arms in *bras bas*.

2 Push off into the air, fully stretching your legs and feet.

3 Come down quietly into *demi-plié* with the left foot in front in 3rd position.

Changements (Boys)

Boys make a quarter turn in the air with each *changement* as a build-up to *tour en l'air*, which is a spring making one or more turns in the air before coming down again. There is a half turn in Grade Three and a whole one in the Senior Grade.

REMEMBER
○ Keep your legs and feet close together as you turn in the air.
○ Lower your heels firmly in *demi-plié*, with your back well supported.

Nicola Katrak as Lise in the Royal Ballet's La Fille Mal Gardée.

⤜GRADE THREE⤚

A difficult grade, full of technical hurdles, but if you can overcome them, you are well on the way to the next grade.

AT THE BARRE

Pliés

Now, at last, *pliés* are taken like a professional dancer, facing sideways to the *barre*. Only one hand rests lightly on the *barre*, slightly in front of the body and with the elbow relaxed, but not bent. As for Grade Two, 1st, 2nd and 3rd positions (or 5th if you can manage it) are used for the *demi-* and *grand-pliés,* but now the free arm will assist the full *plié* with a simple *ports de bras.* This begins in 2nd position of the arms and on the downward movement descends slowly to *bras bas.* On the way up it will be passing through 1st position by the time you have recovered to *demi-plié*, and when you have fully stretched your knees it will be back in 2nd position. If you time it well, it will look as if everything is working together. Your teacher will tell you whether you should include any movement of the head, too.

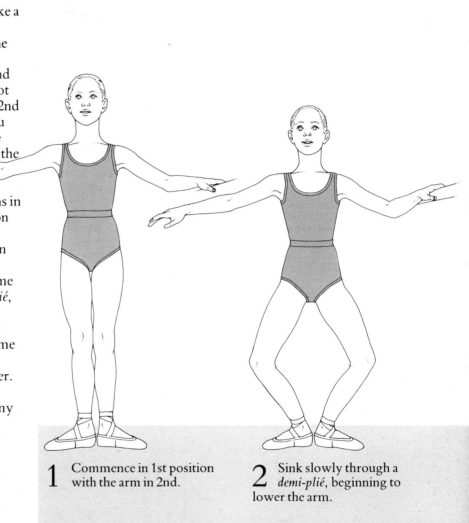

1 Commence in 1st position with the arm in 2nd.

2 Sink slowly through a *demi-plié,* beginning to lower the arm.

Battements Tendus

These are taken *en croix* as in Grade Two, but in a different rhythm, making the movement faster and therefore harder because it must be done with just as much care.

REMEMBER
○ Keep the back well lifted as the arm lowers to *bras bas*.
○ Keep the movement smooth and continuous throughout.
○ Make everything work together for good co-ordination.

3 By the time you reach the bottom of the *grand plié*, the arm will be in *bras bas*.

4 Slowly recover through a *demi-plié*, raising the arm to 1st position.

5 Finally, brace the thighs while fully opening the arm to 2nd position.

Battements Glissés

Do you remember what *glisser* means? In Grade Three the movement is taken *en croix*. It starts from 3rd position (or 5th position if you can manage it) with one hand on the *barre*. Because you are strong enough to do it with more care now, you will find an extra movement on the way in.

1 Slide your foot out as you did in Grade Two, but with more pressure and energy.

2 Place your foot, with control, *à terre* (on the ground).

3 Bring your leg back to 3rd position (or, nearer your examination, 5th position) with pressure through the foot, as in Grade Two, until it arrives home. There is one whole count to hold the close, for if this is not firm the following outward movement will be useless. In case you were not successful the first time, there is a second try in each position *en croix*.

1

Ronds de Jambe à terre

This is a circular movement of one leg, on the ground. When the circle is made outwards, it is called *en dehors*, and when inwards it is called *en dedans*. If you keep your knee turned sideways throughout the circular action, it will help to loosen your leg at the hip joint and further increase your turnout. In this grade this is a preparation only, so there are four counts for each circle.

Ronds de Jambe à terre, en dehors

1 From 1st position, slide your outside leg forwards until your foot is fully pointed (one count).

2 Carry your leg, fully stretched, round to 2nd position, keeping your toes on the ground (one count). Is your knee still equally turned out?

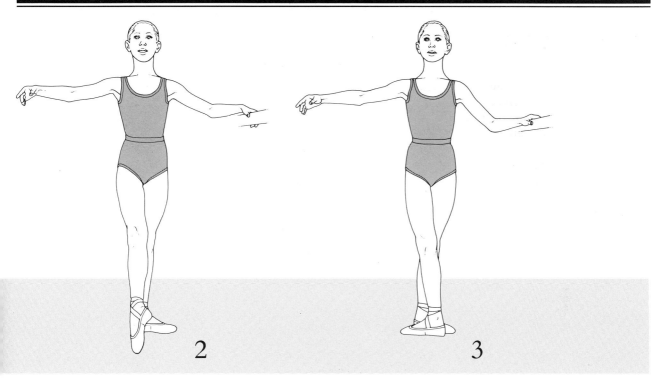

2

3

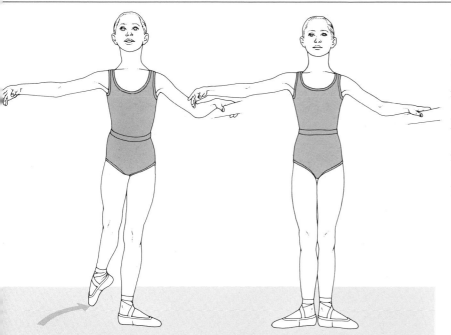

REMEMBER
○ Hold your hips very still — this is an exercise for the leg only!
○ Pull your legs up tightly and keep them evenly turned out.
○ Relax your foot when it arrives in 1st position.
○ Keep your weight over the leg you are standing on.

3 Continue to circle your stretched leg and foot round to the back, toes still on the ground, until your heel is opposite 1st position (one count).

4 Close your foot from the back to 1st position (one count), making sure that it arrives relaxed and without allowing your ankle to drop forwards.

Now try it all the other way round, *en dedans*, taking your leg to the back first. You may find this circle a little more difficult, because your thigh has to work harder to keep your knee facing outwards.

Battements Frappés

Frappé means 'beaten' or 'struck'. This is a new movement. In this grade it is taken from 2nd position as a preparation only to learn the action of the knee and ankle. It will help you to develop quick footwork for steps in the centre.

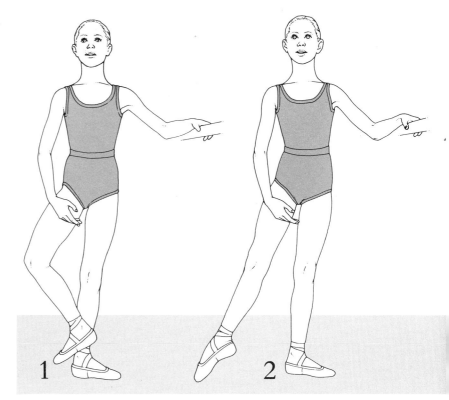

The position that your working foot is brought to, *devant* and *derrière*, is called *cou-de-pied* (neck of the foot). It can be found just above the ankle of the supporting leg.

Retirés

Retiré means 'withdrawn'. This is another new movement and it forms the beginning of a movement called a *développé,* which appears in Grade Four. *Retiré* also appears in a springing step in this grade. Can you discover which one?

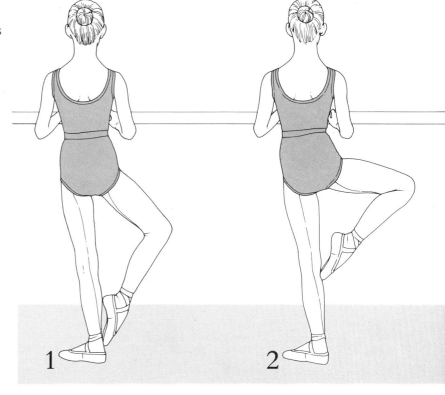

REMEMBER
○ Keep your hips square to the front to make sure that your turnout is even in both legs.

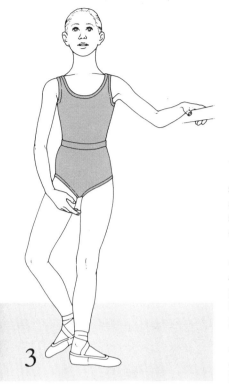

3

1 Start with your working leg *à la seconde*. Keeping your thigh still, bend the leg in at the knee and ankle to a position in front of the supporting leg with your toes just off the floor.

2 Holding your thigh still, place your lower leg back in 2nd position, stretching your knee and ankle firmly, with the toes of your pointed foot resting on the floor.

3 Then fold the working leg in so that the foot is placed *derrière,* or behind, the supporting leg.

REMEMBER
○ Extend your leg firmly from the *cou-de-pied* position, but not so hard that it jars your knee joint. It isn't good for it!
○ Keep your thigh still in 2nd position throughout. Don't let it rise up and down or fall forwards.

3

1 Release one foot from the floor, fully pointed.

2 Draw your thigh up firmly in 2nd position while sliding your pointed toes to the hollow just at the back of your supporting knee.

3 Carefully slide your foot down your supporting leg until the working knee is fully stretched and your foot is back in 5th position.

Sickle foot
Keep your heel forwards in line with your lower leg, both on the way up and on the way down. Otherwise it will form a 'sickle', or twist, at the ankle.

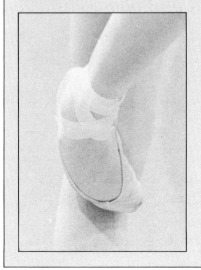

Développés

Développé means 'developed', and the movement is a slow unfolding of one leg. It is practised at the *barre* to gain strength, control and balance, so that in the centre you will be able to unfold the leg into any position and hold it there. The movement is harder to control in 2nd and *derrière*, and therefore it is practised in these positions facing the *barre*, holding on with two hands to help you.

REMEMBER

○ Hold your turnout equally in both thighs.

○ Listen to the music — it will help you with the slow unfolding.

○ Practise it until you can do it with ease. A pained expression is not attractive in a dancer!

Développé à la seconde

1 Starting in 1st position, your working foot slides up the *side* of your supporting leg in order not to lose the turnout of your working thigh. (Where have you made this position before?) The height of your foot will depend on where you can hold your thigh as your leg unfolds.

2 Keeping your thigh still and both hips square to the *barre*, unfold your leg and then lower it as before, closing the foot to 5th position *derrière*. Be careful not to lose any turnout in your thigh on the way down.

1

2

Développé devant

1 Start in 5th position, arm *bras bas*. Raise the front foot until fully pointed and slide it up the front of the supporting leg to a position just below the knee, keeping the thigh in 2nd position.

2 Holding the thigh at the same height, begin to unfold the leg by pushing the lower half forward first so that you keep the turnout already established in the hip joint.

3 Stretch the leg fully in the air taking care to ease the knee into position so that you do not jar the joint. Hold it there for a moment.

4 Keeping the back straight and well lifted, lower the leg slowly until the pointed foot reaches the floor, then close it with pressure to 5th position. Lower your arm to *bras bas* with the closing of the foot.

3

4

Développé derrière

There is one extra thing to learn about the *développé derrière*. This is the first time that you have had to raise and hold your leg so high off the ground. In order to help keep it there, your body tilts slightly forwards as your leg unfolds, and then gradually recovers to an upright position with the lowering. Your teacher will help you find the right amount of tilt, and will make sure that you have not pulled the weight of your body backwards off your supporting leg.

1 From 5th position, draw your working foot up the back of your supporting leg to a position behind the knee with your thigh out to the side.

2 Holding your thigh at the same height, slowly push it backwards as your leg unfolds so that by the time your knee has straightened your leg is directly behind your hip. Unlike *développé devant*, your thigh begins to move backwards *before* the unfolding of the lower half of your leg, in order to keep the turnout already established in your hip joint. Lower and close as before.

1

2

Grands Battements

This is no longer a preparation but the real thing! Starting with your feet in 5th position, if possible, your leg is thrown up and then carefully lowered back to its starting position. It is faster than the other *grands battements* you have learned, taking only one count instead of four, and because this is much more difficult, those to 2nd position and *derrière* face the *barre*.

Devant

Grand battement devant

1 Begin the throwing action with a *battement glissé* movement to make sure that your leg is well stretched and your foot fully arched.

2 Then throw up your foot to loosen your leg at the hip joint.

3 After the throw, lower your leg with control and close, with pressure through your foot, back to 5th position (like the closing of a *battement glissé*).

REMEMBER
○ Throw your working leg *without* disturbing your supporting one.
○ Keep your back still (except to *derrière*, when you are allowed to move it slightly).
○ Keep your knees tight.

Grand battement to 2nd position and derrière

1 *Grand battement* to 2nd position is taken facing the *barre* to help keep your hips and back under control.

2 In *grand battement derrière*, as with *développé derrière*, your body tilts slightly forwards as your leg is thrown, and recovers to an upright position as your leg is lowered. The amount of tilt depends on the height of your throw. Your teacher will help you to place your body correctly.

A la seconde   **Derrière**

Relevés

Relevé means 'lifted' or 'raised up'. The *relevé* movement is taken here from two feet and is done in both 1st and 2nd positions. Because it is a new movement, it will face the *barre*. It will strengthen your legs and feet in preparation for *pointe* work (when special shoes are worn to protect your toes), and is therefore practised only by the girls. Try several *relevés* in 1st position without stopping in between.

1 *Demi-plié* in 1st position.

2 Pushing off your heels, swiftly straighten your knees and draw your feet firmly on to *demi-pointe*, or half-toes, drawing them a little closer together and lifting your body well. Lower both your heels at the same time with a slight spring to 1st position in *demi-plié*, keeping your back still and well supported.

REMEMBER
○ Keep your back still throughout.
○ Keep your heels forwards towards the *barre* on the *relevé* to retain your turnout.
○ Try to hold the turnout at the top of your leg throughout the exercise.
○ Press your knees out over your toes on the downward spring into *demi-plié*.

1 *Demi-plié* as before.

2 *Relevé*, drawing the feet up on to *demi-pointe*. Lower as before, with a slight spring into *demi-plié* in 2nd position.

Relevés in 1st Position

Relevés in 2nd Position

IN THE CENTRE

Ports de Bras

Ports de bras in this grade introduces a sideways bend of the body. Use your arms and hands softly, as if they were being blown by a gentle breeze.

Battements Tendus – en effacé and en écarté

This is an exercise like that done in Grade Two but introducing the *effacé* direction. Also, the *battements tendus* are taken from 5th position instead of 3rd. As you will hear from the music, these *battements tendus* are quicker than they were in Grade Two, but they should still be strong and controlled. Keep your posture firm to help.

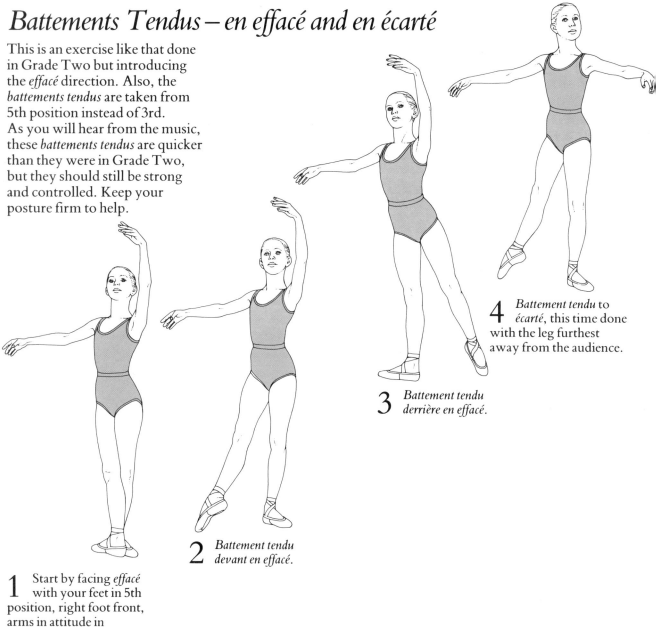

4 *Battement tendu* to *écarté*, this time done with the leg furthest away from the audience.

3 *Battement tendu derrière en effacé.*

2 *Battement tendu devant en effacé.*

1 Start by facing *effacé* with your feet in 5th position, right foot front, arms in attitude in opposition.

Arabesque à terre

An *arabesque* consists of balancing on one leg with the other extended behind, the arms in a position to create the longest oblique, or slanted, line possible between your fingertips and your toes. This has to be done without the aid of your shoulders or hips, which remain square to the line of direction. The oblique line curves slightly at your body and, as usual, your head and eyes provide the finishing touches. *Arabesque* is one of the most well-known positions in ballet. It is usually viewed sideways, or almost sideways, to see the dancer's outline at its best. There are many different *arabesques* that can be performed slowly or quickly as part of a springing step (you will find an example later in this grade). But you will be doing only three of the basic ones here, all taken to the new direction, *en effacé*.

REMEMBER
○ Bring your shoulders forward over your supporting leg on the transfer of your weight.
○ Hold your posture firm.
○ Make the longest line possible without making it look stiff.
○ Feel good!

1 Start with the right foot *devant* in 5th position *en effacé*, arms *bras bas*. To prepare for the *arabesque*, stretch your right leg forwards, raising your arms to 1st position.

2 To make a 1st *arabesque*, push off your back leg until it is stretched with a fully arched foot, stepping on to a well-turned-out, straight supporting leg. Place your right arm forwards in an upwards oblique line, your left arm resting in 2nd position, both palms down. Lift your head and look over your fingertips. Recover to the starting position by opening your front arm to 2nd position, then take both arms to *bras bas* as you close.

3 Prepare for 2nd *arabesque* in the same way by stepping forwards again on to your right leg, this time lifting the arm opposite your supporting leg (the left arm), but not so high that it covers your face. Your right arm will be in 2nd position, palms down, and your shoulders and hips square, head lifted with your eyes looking forward over your front arm. Recover as before.

4 3rd *arabesque* is like putting 1st and 2nd *arabesque* together (1+2=3). Prepare as before, taking your right arm forwards to 1st *arabesque* and the left arm forwards to 2nd *arabesque*, eyes looking over your top arm. In this position, test your balance by raising your leg at the back just a little off the ground. Recover to 5th position. Try it all to the other *effacé* direction, stepping on to the left leg.

Glissades

These are faster than those in Grade Two, having only one count in which to complete the movement. Nevertheless, they still need two stretched feet and a lift in the middle! They are taken from 5th position with the feet changing over on each closing, and can travel sideways to the right or left. If you are good at *glissades*, your arms may be used from 2nd to 3rd position, rather than remaining in *bras bas*.

4 Slide your left foot quickly but firmly into 5th position *devant*, bringing your left arm across to 3rd position and looking over it.

3 Transfer your weight over, taking your arms to 2nd position.

Pas de Chat

This means 'step of the cat', and the movement is so called because of its light, cat-like quality. It can be seen in many of the classical ballets, in particular *The Sleeping Beauty*, where there are two dancers dressed as cats, and in *Swan Lake*, where the four cygnets do a series of sixteen *pas de chats* across the stage. Next time you go to the ballet look out for them. Here they are taken in one count each, travelling diagonally forwards to the right or left.

4 Close your left foot, which should arrive at almost the same time as your right foot, in 5th position *devant*. Straighten both knees immediately.

3 Land quietly on to your right leg, beginning to lower the other.

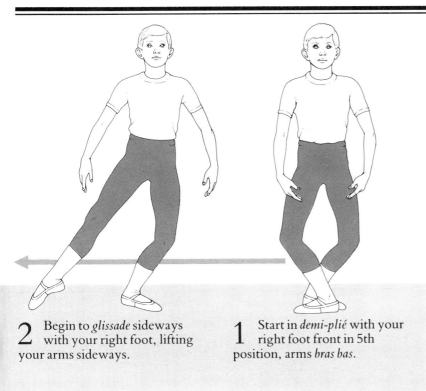

REMEMBER
○ Now that it is faster, put the accent on the closing foot.
○ Try to use your arms softly and gracefully.
○ Maintain the turnout of your legs and good posture.

Repeat the *glissade*, still travelling to the right and starting with your right (now back) foot again. Change your feet over on the closing, and change your arms so that the right one is now forward in 3rd position. Keep practising it to the right and then try it all to the left, starting with your left foot front.

2 Begin to *glissade* sideways with your right foot, lifting your arms sideways.

1 Start in *demi-plié* with your right foot front in 5th position, arms *bras bas*.

REMEMBER
○ Don't just lift your knees to your ears — spring!
○ Keep it quiet, light and stealthy. Study a cat!
○ Make sure that the second foot that lifts to *retiré* is fully pointed.

2 Quickly bend your left leg up to *retiré* as if chasing your right foot with your left.

1 Start in 5th position in *demi-plié*, left foot front, arms in 3rd with your right arm forward. Raise your right leg rapidly to *retiré* while pushing off your left until it is fully stretched in order to give height to your spring.

Practise several *pas de chats*, first with a wait of one count in between each one, and then continuously, in which case each will end in *demi-plié* as there is no time to straighten your legs in between. Do not forget to have a go to the left, starting with the right foot in 5th position *devant*.

Pirouette

In Primary and Grades One and Two you learned how to place a *pirouette*, how to balance there and how to use your head and eyes. Now, at last, it is time to put everything together to try a single turn *en dehors* (do you remember what that means?). It will be preceded by a *relevé* in *pirouette* position (like *relevé* at the *barre* but on one leg), and the turn will finish in an open position to give you some stability at the end. Experienced dancers make many turns in different positions, such as *attitude* and *arabesque*, but no doubt this is how they first learned to *pirouette* too. Have you tried spinning round already?

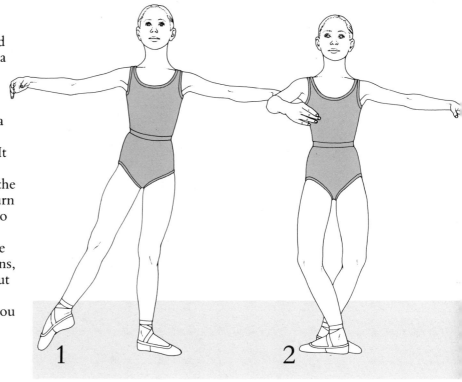

1   2

Preparation (Boys)

Boys have a choice of two positions from which to take this preparation and *pirouette*, either from 2nd position, as in the Grade Two preparation for *pirouette* in the centre (turn back and remind yourself), or from 4th opposite 5th, as on the right.
From then on, *pirouette en dehors* as for the girls, finishing in 4th *en fondu*.

For a turn to the right, take your foot from the side to a small 4th *derrière* (opposite 5th) in *demi-plié*.

REMEMBER
○ Lift your body well on top of your supporting leg.
○ Relax your shoulders.
○ Brace your knee to the side.

Pirouette en dehors (ending in 4th position *en fondu*)
When you make a bend on one leg, it is called *fondu*, which means 'sinking' or 'melting' (rather than *demi-plié*, which involves two bent knees). This downward movement should therefore be soft and spongy. Look back through the earlier grades and see where you have used a *fondu* before (remember, it was not referred to by its French name earlier!)

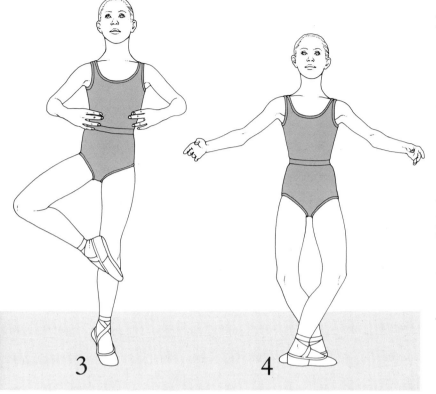

3   4

Preparation (Girls)

1 Open your leg to 2nd position, arms in 2nd.

2 *Demi-plié* in 5th position, taking one arm across to 3rd position.

3 *Relevé* to *pirouette* position, arms in *pirouette* position, holding your thigh firmly out to the side.

4 With a slight spring, close your raised foot to the back in 5th position, opening your arms to *demi-bras*.
Repeat the whole thing to the other side.
Then repeat the first two steps of the preparation and follow them with the sequence below.

1   2   3

1 *Relevé*, pushing up firmly into the turn and making a swift inward movement of your side arm to *pirouette* position. Leave your head and eyes behind.

2 Bring your head and eyes round to the front in advance of your body.

3 Lower into 4th *en fondu en croisé* by placing your raised leg behind your body, keeping your back knee straight and with your supporting foot flat on the ground to anchor you. Open your arms to *demi-bras* to keep your weight forwards over the *fondu*.

Try it all the other way, so that the *pirouette* turns to the left. From time to time practise more than one turn. If you fall over, pick yourself up, dust yourself off and start all over again. It's a little like falling off a horse! Keep trying.

Jetés

The basic spring from one foot to another, plus an elementary exercise for the throwing action of one leg, has been tackled already in Grade Two. Now it is time to put them together!

1 Start in 5th position, left foot front and *demi-plié*.

2 Begin to make a swishing movement, like a *battement glissé*, to 2nd position with your back (right) foot. As your right foot reaches its full extension, push off your supporting leg, using the 'swish' to help you up.

3 Spring into the air, fully pointing your underneath foot and keeping your right leg still.

4 Draw your right leg in on the way down so that on landing it replaces your other foot. Bend your left leg up, thigh to the side and your foot fully pointed behind your calf.

To repeat the *jeté* to the other side, lower your foot to the ground in order to make a *battement glissé* movement to the left, passing through 5th position on the way. Can you do 12 at a time?

REMEMBER

○ Keep your 'swish' under control. The stronger and lower it is the more it will help you up. A *grand battement* movement is only useful if you are going to use the step to travel.

○ Avoid heaving with your arms and back. Keep your top half calm and leave the hard work to your legs and feet.

○ Breathe!

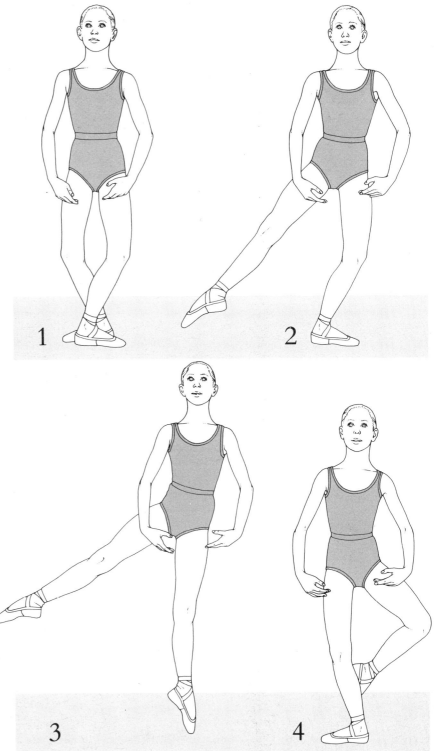

Alain Dubreuil and Marion Tait, principal dancers of Sadler's Wells Royal Ballet, dancing in Elite Syncopations. This is one of MacMillan's most popular concoctions of dances to ragtime tunes; it was first performed by The Royal Ballet in 1974.

Posé Temps Levé in arabesque

Posé means the way in which a dancer steps out, in any direction, into a position. *Temps levé* means raising the body by springing into the air (that is, hopping on one leg). This appears in the set *enchaînement* for this grade and makes use of the 1st *arabesque* that you learned earlier. The important thing to remember about *temps levé* is that it does not change feet.

REMEMBER
○ Make your spring look light and effortless.
○ Use your head and eyes.
○ Dance it!

1 Prepare to step forwards on your left leg (*posé*), arms to 1st position.

2 *Posé* into 1st *arabesque*, bending your left knee in preparation for the hop.

3 Take off from your supporting leg, holding everything else still.

4 Land in *arabesque en fondu*, holding your back firmly so that the line does not begin to collapse. Try combining this step with others.

Margaret Barbieri and David Ashmole starring as Swanilda and Franz in Coppelia.

❧ GRADE FOUR ❧

A more sophisticated grade than Grade Three, requiring more sense of performance.

Pliés

These are taken in the same manner as in Grade Three, with the addition of *demi-plié* in 4th opposite 5th position. Practising this movement will be useful in many ways later on.

The space between your feet should be approximately the length of one foot. You should feel every bit of the underneath surface of your feet on the ground. With your back held upright, place your weight evenly between your feet and keep both heels firmly down in order to fully stretch your muscles.

REMEMBER
○ Not to let your stomach relax or your back may arch.
○ Not to favour one leg by standing further over on it than the other.
○ Not to roll the inner side of your ankles forwards, letting your knees drop forwards with them.
○ Not to look down!

Battements Tendus

Having learned how to execute both slow and quick *battements tendus en croix* in the previous two grades, you are now ready to add a transfer of weight from one leg to two legs and back again. This will be useful in the centre.

Note the slight deviation from the normal sequence *en croix*. Instead of working *devant*, *à la seconde*, *derrière*, the exercise goes from *devant* to *derrière*, and then to *à la seconde*.

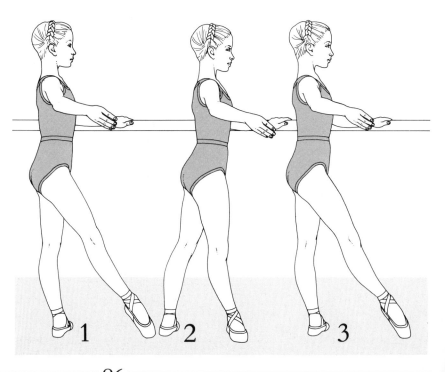

1 Stand in 5th position with one hand resting on the *barre* and the free arm in 2nd position. Stretch your leg *devant*.

2 Lower the heel of your front foot into 4th position, retaining the turnout of your working leg and placing your weight evenly between both feet. Keep your back supported.

3 Fully transfer your weight back on to your original supporting leg by pushing firmly off your front foot. Draw your foot back along the floor to 5th position, arriving with the leg evenly turned out with the supporting one.

4 Slide your inside leg *derrière*, keeping your toes opposite the heel of your supporting leg.

5 Lower your heel to 4th position, placing your weight evenly between your feet and without twisting at the hips so that you achieve the turnout honestly.

6 Transfer your weight back on to your front leg as before. Close your foot to 5th position.

7 Stretch your front leg to 2nd position.

8 Lower your heel carefully through your foot, maintaining an even turnout and with your weight central.

9 Transfer your weight firmly back on to your supporting leg. Slide your foot back into 5th position *devant*.

Battements Glissés

These are taken *en croix* as in Grade Three, but now the music tells you that the movement should be done with a greater sense of urgency and with even better use of your legs and feet. There is a slight pause once the foot is off the ground to test your control and to show off your beautifully stretched feet.

Ronds de Jambe à terre

The circular movement inwards and outwards now starts from a *dégagé à la seconde* (a stretch to 2nd position) and is taken faster than in Grade Three, that is, with only two counts for each circle.

(When you stretch your leg and foot to an open position *devant, à la seconde* or *derrière* without closing it again, it is called a *dégagé*, which means 'disengaged'.)

Battements Frappés

Having learned the basic action in Grade Three, you are now going to add a strike to the movement to develop further strength and flexibility of your feet. This time though, your foot will *start* in the *cou-de-pied* position.

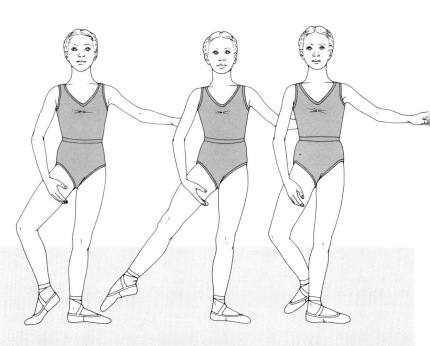

REMEMBER
○ Keep your thigh still, as in Grade Three.
○ Arch your foot fully after the strike.
○ Hold the turnout of your working thigh, particularly when placing your foot in *cou-de-pied derrière*.

1 Starting in *cou-de-pied devant*, extend your leg from your knee, striking the ball of your foot along the ground as it moves.

2 Because of the action used for the strike, your foot will finish just off the ground in 2nd position, like a *battement glissé*.

3 When your foot returns to *cou-de-pied*, it will do so without touching the floor because the striking only happens on the outward movement. Alternate the *cou-de-pied* positions as for Grade Three.

Développés

These are taken *en croix* as in Grade Three, but sideways to the *barre* and with the unfolding movement from a *retiré* position throughout.

Exercise for Attitude

An *attitude* is a balletic position that is said to have been invented by Blasis, who was inspired by the statue of Mercury by Giovanni da Bologna. This is a preparatory exercise only for *attitude derrière*. It will not appear again until the Senior Grade, where one of the springing steps ends in *attitude*.

REMEMBER
○ Keep your knee higher than your foot.
○ Keep the weight of your body over your supporting leg.
○ Keep your head poised.

1 Place your working foot in *cou-de-pied derrière*.

2 Holding your knee at the same angle, push your thigh away from your body and raise your leg. Allow your body to tilt slightly forwards.

Grands Battements

These are taken as in Grade Three, with one count for each, but sideways to the *barre* throughout, in a series *en croix*.

IN THE CENTRE

Ports de Bras

In Grade Four, *ports de bras* involves the use of *épaulement*, which means 'shouldering'. It is used to give a position or movement a different look or line, and consists of turning your body from your waist upwards in order to bring one shoulder further forward than the other. You will meet this again in the *arabesque* exercise. Try to keep both shoulders and arms relaxed in *épaulement*, so that they will be pleasing and attractive to the eye.

Pas de Bourrée

This means 'step of the *bourrée*', an eighteenth-century dance. These are running steps and there are more than 28 varieties! But don't worry — we are going to study only the two which are required for Grade Four! *Pas de bourrées* are a very important part of a dancer's vocabulary. They can be used in series to give speed and neatness in footwork; they can be used as 'linking' steps in *enchaînements*. They can also be used as 'spring-board' steps leading into big jumps. To add to their versatility, they can also be taken turning and on full *pointe*. Good use of the legs and a well-poised body (no sitting in the hips!) are essential if lightness and speed are to be achieved. Practise the *pas de bourrées* in two counts until you can do them correctly. Then gradually increase the speed until you are able to skim along the floor without losing neatness and accuracy.

REMEMBER
○ Keep your thighs evenly turned out throughout.
○ Keep your posture firm and well supported.
○ Take care, if using *épaulement*, to keep your hips and feet *en face*.

Pas de Bourrée—Over
(This always starts with the back foot.)
Travelling to the left:

1 Start in 5th position, left foot *devant*, arms *bras bas*. *Dégagé* your right foot to 2nd position *à terre en fondu*. Count: and . . .

2 Keeping your right knee straight, draw your leg in to 5th position, rising on to both *demi-pointes*. Count: one.

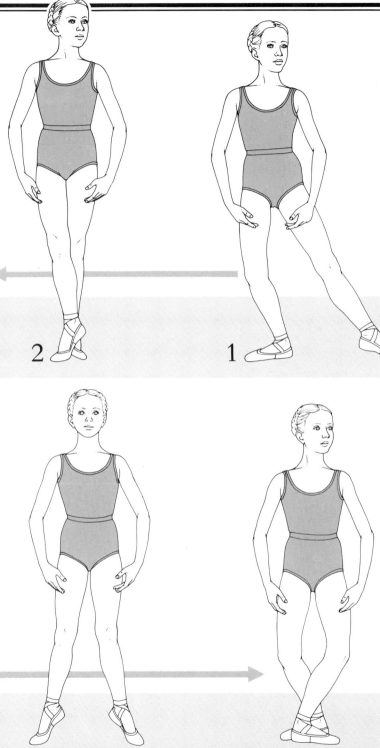

2 **1**

3 Step to the side on your left foot, still on *demi-pointe*. Count: and . . .

4 Close your right foot to 5th *derrière* as you lower gently into *demi-plié*. Count: two. Note the use of your head and *épaulement* for added interest.

Pas de Bourrée — Under

(This always starts with the front foot.)
Travelling to the right:

1 Start with your left foot *devant* in 5th position. Extend your front foot to 2nd *en fondu* as before. Count: and . . .

2 Draw your left leg into 5th *derrière*, rising on to *demi-pointe*. Count: one.

3 Step to 2nd position with your right foot. Count: and . . .

4 Lower gently into *demi-plié* as you draw your left foot into 5th position *devant*. Count: two.

Next, change your feet over and travel the movement to the left instead. Say to yourself, 'behind, side, front'. Note that for both *pas de bourrées* the working foot always finishes in the position in which it started.
Now try *pas de bourrée* 'over' followed by one 'under', in a series. When you can perform them efficiently, try them in one count each ('and a one'). You will find the quicker version in one of your set *enchaînements*.

Change feet and try starting *pas de bourrée* 'over' with your right foot *devant*, travelling to the right. Say quietly to yourself 'front, side, behind'. Count: one and two.

Arabesque Epaulée

The exercise in this grade uses 1st and 2nd *arabesques* from Grade Three and adds *arabesque épaulée* (*épaulée* means 'shouldered'). It is taken to the *croisé* direction, and in each case the *arabesque* leg is raised *en l'air*. Do not forget that the higher your leg goes the further forward your body has to tilt, not only to keep the line but to act as a counter–balance. When your body is tipped right over — with your arm low and your leg high — it is called *arabesque penchée* (*penchée* means 'tilted').

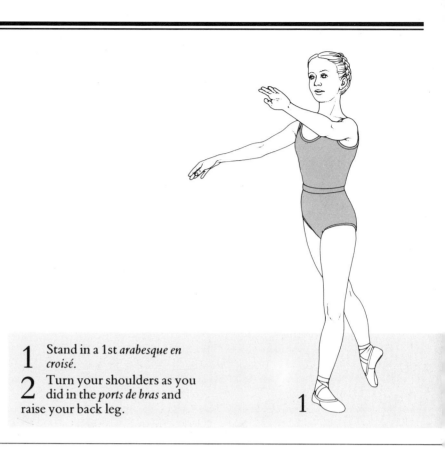

1 Stand in a 1st *arabesque en croisé*.

2 Turn your shoulders as you did in the *ports de bras* and raise your back leg.

Assemblés

This means 'assembled' or 'brought together', and it is a jump which takes off from one leg and lands on two. Because it is difficult you are given two counts in which to practise the *assemblé*, although it is normally performed in one when linked to other steps. Like *pas de bourrées*, it can be taken 'over' or 'under'. Try several together, keeping your arms in *bras bas*.

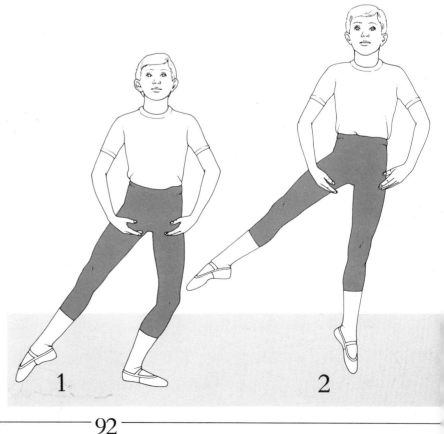

2

REMEMBER
○ Maintain the turnout in your supporting leg as well as in the other.
○ Keep your hips square when making the *épaulée* movement.
○ Poise your head well.

Pirouette

This is taken in the same setting as Grade Three but with a turn EACH time instead of the *relevé* preparation to *pirouette* position. Have a look back to remind yourself.

3   **4**

Assemblés — Over

1 As usual, start in *demi-plié* in 5th position, left foot *devant*. *Battement glissé* to 2nd position with your back foot, beginning to push up from the *fondu* towards the end.

2 Helped by the force of your extension, spring high into the air, fully stretching your left leg and foot.

3 As you come down, pull your right leg across your left, drawing one foot in front of the other (the *assemblé*).

4 Lower through your feet and legs into *demi-plié* in 5th position. Stretch your knees and then *demi-plié* to repeat it with the left foot, coming over to the front.

Assemblés — Under

Start with your right foot *devant* and repeat the movement, extending your front foot to the side and closing it *derrière* on landing.

REMEMBER
○ Spring as high as possible to give yourself time to assemble the feet BEFORE landing.
○ Keep your posture particularly well supported to help you to spring.
○ Control your arms — they may try to help you up!

Senior Grade is the highest of the grades. The way in which the exercises and steps have been combined should encourage you to show the technical skills that you have acquired, along with a heightened sense of rhythm and musicality, well co-ordinated movement and, most important of all, your love of dancing.

AT THE BARRE

Pliés

These are now taken in a different combination and should be performed with increasing control and co-ordination.

Battements Tendus

(with transfer of weight)
In this grade you are going to add a *demi-plié* to the transfer of weight you learned in Grade Four.

Repeat this movement *en arrière* ('moving backwards') then *à la seconde*, transferring your weight *back* on to your supporting leg instead of placing it over the working leg.

1 Starting from 5th position with the free arm in 2nd, stretch your free leg firmly *devant*.

2 Lower into a *demi-plié* in 4th position, transferring your weight evenly between your legs.

3 *Dégagé* the back foot *derrière*, transferring your weight firmly on to your front leg (or *en avant*, that is, 'moving forwards'). Close your back foot into 5th position.

94

Battements Glissés

Having practised this in four counts *en croix* in Grade Four, you are ready to end the movement that is taken in two counts in *demi-plié* and to try it on straight legs in one count. This preparation is getting much closer to what you will actually do when you execute the movement in steps in the centre. It faces the *barre* and starts in 5th position.

REMEMBER
○ To keep your lower back upright as you lower into *demi-plié*, or you will begin to lose the turnout in your thighs.
○ To keep your leg low in those movements taken in one count, since this is where you are likely to lose control.

1 When taken in two counts, the foot extends from 5th position *devant* to 2nd position on the first count.

2 Close your foot firmly to 5th position *derrière* on the second count, at the same time lowering carefully into *demi-plié*. Keep alternating the position of your working foot as you repeat the movement. As you have been practising *battements glissés* since Grade 2, it should be developing into a stronger, more controlled exercise by now. Note how the quality of the music has helped throughout.

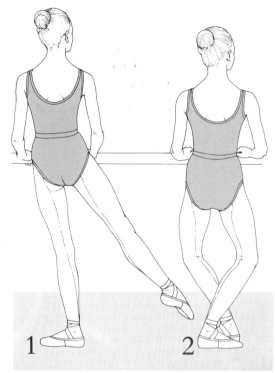

Ronds de Jambe à terre

These start *à la seconde* as in Grade Four, but now each circular movement takes just one count. They are executed *en dehors* and *en dedans*, and are combined with other movements in the set exercise.

Battements Frappés

These are still taken to 2nd position only, but in different counts to Grade Four.

Grands Battements

As for Grade Four, but in a different rhythm so that there is equal emphasis on the throw and the closing. The professional dancer on the right has thrown his leg to its full height!

Développés

The correct way to unfold your leg was fully learned in Grade Four. In this grade there is a whole count set aside for the extension of your leg in the air to show the strength that you have acquired. By now there will also be an increase in the height of your *développé*. This involves lifting your thigh from the *retiré* position before holding it in place to unfold the lower half of your leg.

If you go to the ballet you will see professional dancers taking this movement into many different positions and directions, apparently without any effort!

Entrechat Quatre

Entrechat means 'interweaving' or 'braiding', and *quatre* means 'four'. This is a step, but it is taken at the *barre* at present, to help you to do it correctly. It consists of a spring into the air while making rapid beating movements with both legs. The full name of the *entrechat* depends on the total number of movements made by both legs — in this case two each, or four (*quatre*) altogether.

Entrechat quatre was made famous by a French ballerina called Madame Camargo, who shortened her dress and revealed her ankles in order to show how well she could do beats. Showing your ankles was considered to be very unladylike in the eighteenth century!

1 Start in 5th position, right foot front. Spring into the air, opening your legs slightly sideways.

2 Beat your legs together, crossing your left leg in front.

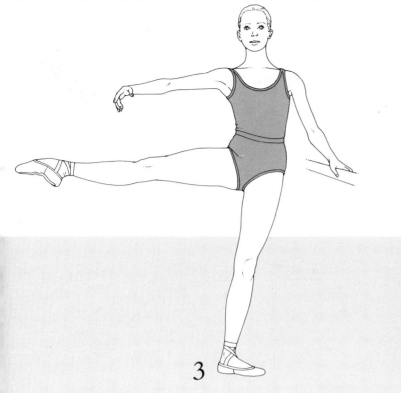

3

Développé to 2nd position

1 Start in 5th position. Draw your front foot up to *retiré*.

2 Lift your thigh without disturbing your hips.

3 Holding your thigh still, unfold the lower half of your leg.

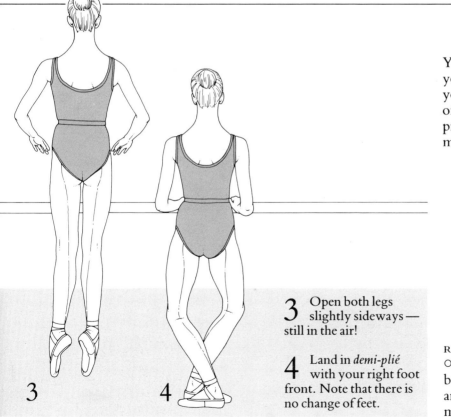

Your teacher will probably give you a few easier exercises to help you with the sideways opening of the legs in the air, in preparation for the beating movement.

3 Open both legs slightly sideways — still in the air!

4 Land in *demi-plié* with your right foot front. Note that there is no change of feet.

REMEMBER
o Open your legs *sideways* to beat, to maintain your turnout and help the speed of the crossing movements.

3   **4**

IN THE CENTRE
Ports de Bras

This is no longer practised as a separate movement but incorporated into the other exercises.

Arabesque

For the girls, *arabesque* is no longer practised alone but introduced into the set *adage* and taken from a *développé* movement. The boys' set *adage* also contains an *arabesque en l'air,* which is moved round on one spot by a series of pivots on the supporting leg. (*Adage* is that part of the class where slow, flowing, controlled movements are combined to develop grace, sense of line, balance [particularly on one leg] and the co-ordination of movements which will later be danced. Like the *enchaînements*, an *adage* can be set, as in the Senior Grade, or free, the combination of movements being put together by the teacher or examiner.)

Pirouette en dehors

Girls Prepared from a *relevé* in 5th position in place of the *dégagé*, and combined with *échappés relevés* to 2nd position.

Boys Prepared from a rise and *demi-plié* in 4th opposite 5th, and finished in both 4th and 5th positions.

Pirouette en dedans

This is introduced for the first time in both the boys' and girls' set *adage*. Your teacher will assist you in building up the preparation for a turn. Precede the preparatory position for 'take off' with a *pas de bourrée* 'under', placing your closing foot forward into 4th position *en fondu en croisé* instead of *demi-plié* in 5th position. Your arms will arrive in 3rd position, same arm forward as your front leg. This is how it is combined in the set *adage*.

1 Place your weight well forward over the *fondu*.

2 Release your back foot and carry your leg round *en l'air* to a low 2nd position, bringing your body and supporting foot *en face* at the same time. Open your front arm to 2nd.

3 *Relevé* into *pirouette* position, bringing your left arm across your body to form a *pirouette* position with the other and spin! Spring your feet into 5th in *demi-plié*.

1

An arabesque! Which one is it?

2   3

REMEMBER
○ Lift your body upright as your leg arrives in 2nd position.
○ Whip your foot from 2nd into *pirouette* position on the *relevé* and find your 'spot'.
○ Keep your weight forward and central over your supporting leg.

Pas de Bourrée Piqué (Girls only)

Piqué means 'pricked'. This step has a quite different quality to the *pas de bourrées* learned in Grade Four, and is most effective when performed on full *pointe*. Here it is danced *en demi-pointe* to a minuet rhythm to give equal emphasis to each movement and a light, crisp quality to the action of your legs and feet.

1 Start in 5th position, right foot front with arms in *demi-seconde*. *Fondu* on your right leg, lifting your left foot to *cou-de-pied derrière*.

2 Step on to your left *demi-pointe*, straightening your knee and immediately place your right foot under your supporting knee, toes fully stretched and thigh pressed out to the side.

3 Step to the side on to your right foot and immediately bring your left foot, fully stretched, under your knee, keeping your thigh well turned out.

4 Lower on to your left foot as if closing to 5th position in *demi-plié*, at the same time releasing the right foot to *cou-de-pied derrière*. Arms are now in 3rd position (same arm forwards as the front foot) with the use of *épaulement*.

Repeat it travelling the other way, moving the arms smoothly from 3rd to 3rd. Remember to keep your hips and feet *en face*.

Assemblés

These are now taken in both one and two counts, and combined with other steps. Look back to Grade Four to remind yourself of the details.

Dierdre Eyden, Fiona Chadwick, Bryony Brind and Wayne Eagling of The Royal Ballet dancing in Balanchine's classic version of Apollo, which he originally created for the New York City Ballet.

Grand Jeté (en avant)

This is done only by boys in this syllabus, but it would do girls no harm to try it, too. It is a big leap forwards from one leg to the other. The position that the body, arms and legs assume during the leap in the air varies. Here it is taken in 2nd *arabesque*.

2   Having made an arc in the air (look opposite), land softly and with control on to your turned-out front leg, keeping the 2nd *arabesque* and holding your back firmly. Having completed the exercise try it with the other leg, travelling in the same direction.

1   Precede the leap with two runs, right, left. Throw your right leg forwards and up like a *grand battement*, at the same time pushing off your back leg and thrusting your weight forwards. Arms are to 1st position. Leap high into the air, like an arrow being shot from a bow, taking your arms to 2nd *arabesque* and stretching your back leg fully.

Tour en l'air

This is a turn (or turns!) in the air, and is very much a male dancer's step. If you remember, there was a preparation for this in Grades Two and Three. Turn back and see if you can find out where.

1   Start *demi-plié* in 5th position, right foot *devant*. Spring straight up into the air, turning your body to the right (*en dehors*). Keep your body forward over your feet and your legs held tightly together. 'Spot' your eyes as for a *pirouette*.

2   Whip the head to the right and find your 'spot' again.

3   Land in *demi-plié* with the *left foot devant*, maintaining good posture. The point at which the foot changes in the air will depend on each individual dancer.

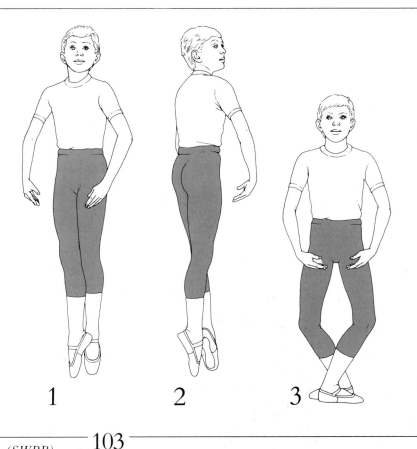

Roland Price in Ashton's Les Rendezvous, (SWRB).

Sissonnes

This is introduced for the first time in this grade. It is not clear where the name of this step came from, although several suggestions are made by the writers of ballet dictionaries. The step itself has a scissor-like quality and is therefore sometimes referred to by dancers as *pas de ciseaux*. There are different types of *sissonnes* — those that take off from two feet and alight on one, like *sissonne ordinaire* ('ordinary') and *sissonne ouverte* ('open'), and those from two feet, that also finish on two feet like *sissonne fermée* ('closed'). They can be taken to any direction.

Sissonne Ordinaire
Devant

1 Start in 5th position, right foot *devant*. Spring into the air, keeping both legs tightly together, with your front foot covering the back one. Raise your arms to 1st position.

2 Land *en fondu* on your back leg, raising your front foot, fully stretched, under your supporting knee. Arms should be in 3rd position, opposite arm to the raised leg in front.

This can be done *derrière* by raising the back leg on landing, with the arms in 3rd position, forward arm again opposite the raised leg.

Sissonne Fermée
(*en avant* only)

1 Start in 5th position, right foot *devant*. Spring up and diagonally forwards, keeping your legs tightly together as for *ordinaire* and raising your arms forwards. Land on your right leg *en fondu*, separating and raising your back leg into an *arabesque* line, arms in 3rd *arabesque* (the arms are shown as they are used in the syllabus, but may be placed in other positions).

2 Close your raised leg immediately into *demi-plié*, holding your arms still. Remember to keep this leg turned out as it lowers, and to keep your posture firm.

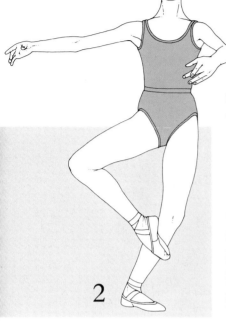

Sissonne Ouverte
(*en avant* only)

1   As for *sissonne fermée*, but instead of closing into 5th in *demi-plié*, hold your raised leg in position and leave your supporting leg *en fondu*. The drawing illustrates the final position of the *sissonne ouverte* in the Girl's Solo Variation. Note that it is taken to the *croisé* direction and is in *attitude*.

Sissonne Ouverte Changée
(*en avant* only)

Changée means 'changed', and refers to a change of feet.

1   From the *demi-plié*, spring up and forwards as for *sissonne fermée*, arms in 1st position.

2   Land on your *back* leg *en fondu*, sweeping the *front* leg back and up into position, arms in *attitude*.

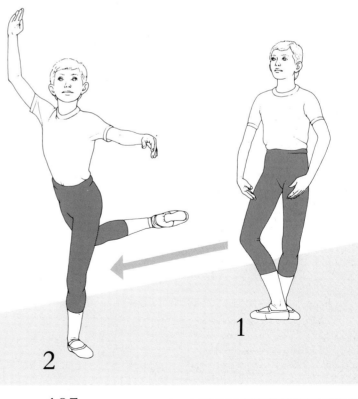

INTERNATIONAL DANCERS

ANTHONY DOWELL
THE ROYAL BALLET

When I was very young I had no ambition to become a ballet dancer, but I was certain that I wanted to be involved with the theatre in some way. I was lucky to have the opportunity to dance, sing and act on a 'real' stage during my early years at my first school, and it was this opportunity that made me realize that I had to be part of the fascinating backstage world. My first teacher advised my parents to send me to a school that concentrated on ballet training as she saw I had a natural gift for classical dancing. Although I was not that keen on dancing I saw it as my 'path' into the world I

wanted, and so I began the long, unexpected and hardworking journey, not just to the theatre but to the grandeur of the Royal Opera House, which, for the past 23 years, has become my 'home' stage.

During my years of never-ending learning, there came a time when my ability and enjoyment of dancing were replaced by the surprise, and sometimes shock, of how hard the work was. I had no idea at the start that so much strength and stamina was needed to dance a solo, let alone a three–act ballet. To this day it is still my biggest fear that I will not have enough energy. I would not be honest if I did not tell you that the days when you feel you are dancing the way you want to are far outnumbered by the days when you feel exhausted and unable to achieve or maintain your personal best. But the rewards and joy of a good performance when it happens, are indescribable; to have danced well in front of a responsive audience is worth all the years of hard work.

MARILYN JONES
THE AUSTRALIAN BALLET

I first started going to ballet when I was five years old, because I walked around on tiptoes. I had difficulty putting my heels down on the floor and it

was suggested by an aunt that ballet would help me to walk properly by stretching the backs of my legs.

I was very shy and learning ballet helped me to overcome this. I made a lot of friends at the ballet studios because I shared the same interests as my classmates. We took part in festivals and concerts, and, apart from the competitive side of it, we had a lot of fun together.

My first professional experience was as an extra in *The Firebird* with The Royal Ballet Company. I was very excited and thrilled to be stepping on to the stage at the famous Covent Garden – my dreams had come true.

Since then I have performed with various ballet companies and have had the marvellous opportunity, through ballet, to visit and perform in many countries. With the Royal Ballet I toured America, and with the Borovansky Ballet I toured throughout my own country, Australia, and New Zealand. I joined the Marquis de Cuevas Company in Paris, and travelled throughout Europe. I've also danced with the London Festival Ballet. In the Australian Ballet, where I spent most of my career, I have been on many tours, including one through South East Asia which was very exciting. If you like travel, ballet is a great way of seeing fascinating places.

I now teach children ballet and love this very much – it is a privilege to be able to pass on my knowledge of dance which originally had been passed on to me. I am also Artistic Director of Sydney City Ballet Company, a young company which provides performances for school children as well as evening performances. Australia is a large country with many country towns, and the company tours throughout New South Wales, taking ballet to country areas which otherwise wouldn't have the opportunity to see ballet on stage.

It has been wonderful to work with famous dancers and choreographers all over the world. The hard work has been more than repaid by the applause and appreciation of the audiences. To be able to give pleasure to so many people is, for me, the most important and rewarding aspect of performing.

PHYLLIS SPIRA – CAPAB BALLET COMPANY, SOUTH AFRICA
I started dancing when I was four years old and I can remember that right from the start I loved the

classes, the discipline and the feeling of moving to music. My mother says that if she were late in taking me to ballet class I would be impatiently waiting at the gate all dressed up and ready to go, furious with her because I would miss the start of the class! As I got older I realized how hard you had to work but I still loved it. Now I know that it becomes even harder as you go along, not easier, but that's all part of the enjoyment.

Dancing is not all about adulation and praise. When I was at the Royal Ballet School, I

trained for my Advanced RAD exam with Miss Edwards, and I only had about five weeks to prepare for it. She was marvellous and a great teacher. When I got to Holland Park for the exam – I was very nervous – the other three candidates did not turn up at all, so I had to do my Advanced all on my own. It was absolutely terrifying. I was sure I had failed! About two weeks later the dreaded envelope arrived from the RAD and I was so scared I just couldn't open it. My room mate had to open it and tell me the result: Honours! I just couldn't believe it. I rushed to the Ballet School, envelope in hand, to find Miss Edwards and tell her the good news. When I found her she said: 'Oh, Honours, well I don't know how'. I was quite upset and deflated, and walked back home thinking that this was indeed a hard life.

It is a hard life, perhaps the hardest of all the performing arts, but the rewards are definitely worthwhile. If you are dedicated and can still enjoy what you do after 25 years of professional dancing, that is something to treasure. I would say to any young person who wants to make a career in ballet that they must want to do it so much, so badly, that *nothing* will stop them from achieving their aims.

I have always enjoyed my work, although actually it hasn't really seemed like work – rather, a way of being paid for doing something I love! Practising every day and the discipline it has brought to my whole life has made me very happy and fulfilled. I always remember a particularly apt cartoon, in which Snoopy from Peanuts says: 'To dance is to live, to live is to dance'. I can honestly say that that has been true for me. If I don't do class for one day, something vital is missing from my life.

PETER SCHAUFUSS
ARTISTIC DIRECTOR OF THE LONDON FESTIVAL BALLET

I was born into the ballet, but this didn't mean that I *had* to become a dancer. In fact, for a few years I wanted to be several other things, including a footballer and a racing driver. I've still got a few scars from my attempts at these sports!

My mother, Mona Vangsaae, was a ballerina with the Royal Danish Ballet in our home town of Copenhagen. My father, Frank Schaufuss, was a principal dancer and, later, Director of the company. So you can imagine, my life was centred around the theatre and the ballet school situated high up under its roof. From our earliest years we students were involved in theatre life, often appearing in the great Danish ballets such as *La Sylphide* and *Napoli*. By the time I was eight or nine I had toured America with the company and had also appeared as the Page in Sir Frederick Ashton's *Romeo and Juliet*, in which my mother created the role of Juliet.

Growing up in a theatre which had for years encouraged male dancers, and joining in productions right from the start, made dancing seem like a perfect job. Of course, it is a very special job, and requires the fitness and

stamina of an athlete, together with the intelligent thinking and feeling of an artist. It also requires a special discipline, and I can see very clearly now how important my early classes were, even if I sometimes thought them a bit boring at the time!

As a busy international dancer I have to be very organized and strict with myself in order to find time in my hectic travel schedule for my ballet classes, as well as my own exercises which I do every day, without fail, before class. Whether I do them in a hotel room or in a city park (where I often get some very funny looks from passers-by!) I make sure they are done.

I have a few grumbles about my life as a dancer – such as living out of a suitcase and travelling endlessly – but the rewards outweigh these. I have had ballets created for me by great choreographers such as George Balanchine; I have danced with all the great ballerinas of today; and I have been able to pay back a little of what I owe to my Danish tradition by producing my own versions of *La Sylphide* and *Napoli* for companies all over the world. Apart from the dancing itself, I think this gives me the greatest pleasure.

GARTH WELCH
THE AUSTRALIAN BALLET

I did not consciously choose to start dancing – it just happened. I had a bad history of bronchial trouble and the doctor suggested that exercise would be good for me. When I was young there were not the clubs available for children to do gymnastics as there are today, but there was a local ballet school and I was sent there. I must say that I am very glad because I have been in good health ever since. I believe the discipline of dance and performing is healthy for both mind and body.

My first teacher, Phyllis Danaher, made a strong impression on me and I can still hear in my mind, all these years later, many of the things she said to me. She made me enjoy working hard in the classroom and, at the same time, the yearly performances she put on made me very much want to be on stage.

I was encouraged to act and to use my voice on stage. I think this is important because many classical dancers now concentrate on the technical side of the art and sometimes forget to act while they dance. Acting and using my voice proved to be particularly important to me, because the last time I performed on stage was as Zach in *A Chorus Line*, in which I had to dance, act and sing. It was a part I loved playing. But my favourite role was Albrecht in *Giselle*, because of the challenge it gave me to create a believable character while having to dance well at the same time.

RICHARD CRAGUN
STUTTGART BALLET
When did I decide to take up dancing? I didn't. Dancing took me up and, happily, it has not put me down for the past 33 years. Ever since I could remember, every time I heard music and saw an open space, it was in that space that I had to be, spinning, leaping and darting from one pose to another. At first it was improvised, of course. I didn't know anything about style or technique. That would have been rather a lot to expect of a six-year-old. And, judging from the number of broken lamps and

chairs in my parents' living room, my judgement of that 'open space' wasn't very accurate, either. So, shortly after this time, the wooden floors of home were replaced by those of my local dancing school and from that time onwards I knew that this was the world for which I had been born.

The love of, and impulse to, dance must be there from birth. They cannot be learned. These, together with talent. As long as you have these three things you will be prepared for the other side of the dance profession, namely: hard work and sacrifice. Although dancing appears to be light and carefree, to achieve a fulfilling career in this field demands a considerable amount of hard work, discipline and dedication.

The rewards, however, are also great, for through the discipline and physical preparation you benefit from not only being aware of how important physical health is but also learn a little more about yourself each day.

Back on the other side again: yes, the applause is wonderful;

the dressing room may be filled with admiring fans; and a few dancers do earn far more than the average salary. But I've always found it a bit odd that I'm being paid for doing something I love so much which I have been doing from the very beginning of my life. Strange world, isn't it? Would you ever think of paying a fish to swim or a bird to fly?

JENNIFER PENNEY
THE ROYAL BALLET
I have always loved, and have always felt deeply moved by, music. For me, dancing is the ideal way of being able to express that love.

I started late for a dancer, when I was 11 years old. I am grateful for that because I had a very normal and carefree childhood. I think it is best not to take ballet very seriously at too young an age.

Although the rewards are many if you are lucky enough to succeed – and luck is just as important as talent – there is a lot of work, disappointment and pain involved. There is very little time for anything else in your life and there is the very real danger that you will have nothing to replace ballet with when your career is over. I think it is, therefore, tremendously important to have interests other than ballet. Whenever I get the chance I paint in watercolours. It is something I'll be able to do, even when I'm 90.

Apart from good health I believe a sense of humour is absolutely *essential* – being able to laugh at yourself is a great life (and face) saver! Having been with the Royal for 20 years, I now look forward to a less strenuous future. When I'm about 40 I think I might exchange my pirouettes for a little farming!

HOW TO FIND A BALLET SCHOOL

Every parent can learn a lesson from Margot Fonteyn's mother. When she and Margot were on their way to China they spent a few months in America. Naturally Margot wanted to keep up with her ballet training, but they knew no-one in Louisville, where they were staying. So Margot was taken to the first dance school listed in the telephone book. Fortunately her mother stayed to watch the class and was horrified to see that it consisted of a few badly organized ballet movements, together with a lot of high kicks and splits. They never went back.

Never take a chance when looking for a school and a teacher. At worst, actual physical damage can result from bad teaching, at best young dancers with potential will become bored and want to give up. Sadly, even now, after years of experience, there are still teachers who ignore boys, or allow girls to dance on *pointe* years too early, ruining their feet.

If you are not able to take advice from someone you know and trust about your local dance schools, you can ask for a list of schools from one of the big teaching and examining organizations such as the Royal Academy of Dancing or the Imperial Society of Teachers of Dancing. Useful information, as well as advertisements, appear in magazines such as *The Dancing Times* in Britain, or the American *Dance Magazine*. Teachers are listed with their experience and qualifications, though it is still worthwhile taking the precaution of watching a class, as there are teachers who acquired their qualifications many years ago and who have not taken the trouble to keep up-to-date with modern methods and ideas. Most reputable schools will be more than happy to let you see a class of the right level and age-group, and there may well be a chance to see the school Christmas show or demonstration. From these it is fairly easy to judge the overall standard of the school as well as the general appearance of the pupils. It is important that they look happy and relaxed when performing.

If you are able to see a class you should note what the room is like as well as the teaching standard. A good non-slip floor is essential and the studio should be light and airy. The number of pupils in the class should ideally be around 15 to 20. If pupils are packed in they have neither the room to move nor the chance of sufficient individual attention from the teacher.

The grooming and appearance of the teacher is just as important as that of the pupils, as they are bound to be influenced by her or him. Watch keenly for how much individual care children get and how much sympathetic correction. Too many teachers set a step or *enchaînement* and then just sit back and watch it. Too much correction can be bad in the early years when pupils should dance largely for fun and to build up stamina and rhythmic ability, but the time soon comes when the poise of the head, the placing of the body and the pointing of the feet are absolutely essential and should constantly be watched for by the teacher.

For many years ballet classes were accompanied by very uninspiring music. But nowadays, teachers are much more likely to use music which is of the correct tempo, and with which children can identify and enjoy dancing to. Musical appreciation should be a part of the training, and classes should not be regimented to strict tempo music. Live music is invariably best, but there may be difficulties in arranging it. There are many good quality tapes made specially for class by leading ballet pianists and teachers, but the stopping and starting can interrupt the pace of the class.

Having chosen a school it is difficult to know exactly how much you should be paying. As with many other purchases it is not necessarily the most expensive which is best, nor will the cheapest always be worst. The extra money may go towards unnecessary facilities and not on the teaching, whilst the cheapest may have the most talented teacher. This has to be a matter of personal judgement.

DRESSING FOR DANCE

Like many other professions, dance has a uniform of its own. Very young dance students, just taking their first steps and learning to enjoy movement, should wear comfortable, almost everyday, clothes: full skirted dresses for girls and shorts for boys. As they develop they will soon need to wear a leotard to give the necessary freedom of movement. The leotard has been the accepted practice costume for dancers since it was invented by Monsieur Leotard in France over a hundred years ago.

HOW TO CHOOSE A LEOTARD

The correct measurement is essential and should be done in a specialist shop by an experienced assistant. If you wish to take the measurement yourself you must measure the exact girth by placing the end of a tape measure on one shoulder, bringing it down the front of the body, between the legs, and back up to the same shoulder. This gives you the correct size of leotard to buy. A leotard which is too small will be uncomfortable and will restrict movement, but even more importantly, if it is too large the outline of the body will be obscured and the teacher may miss

faults in placing and movement. It is very tempting to buy a leotard with growing room, but it is a temptation which should be resisted.

WHERE TO BUY SHOES AND HOW TO FIT THEM

Some local shoe shops stock ballet shoes, but it is best to go to one of the specialist dance shops. As ballet shoes are designed to fit like a second skin it is essential that they are

fitted properly and, once again, that you should *not* allow any growing room. Girls' shoes are made of satin or kid leather and are held on with satin or nylon ribbons. Boys' shoes are made of kid leather or canvas, usually black, and held on with a narrow elastic which should not be too tight. The photographs below show where to attach the ribbon (which comes in one length and must be cut into four equal parts) or

elastic, and how to tie them neatly so that there are no untidy bows or loose ends, which not only get in the way of working efficiently but also look ugly and ruin the line of a stretched foot.

Kind relatives are often tempted to buy ballet shoes, particularly satin ones, as presents, but it would be better if they sent the money instead. Fitting your shoes needs expert guidance, and mistakes made early on can cause problems in the future. This is even more important when girls progress to *pointe* work, around the age of 11. Finding the right *pointe* shoes can be a very difficult business and may take visits to more than one specialist manufacturer. It may even be necessary to have your shoes specially made. The cost of this service is not as great as you might think, as the *pointe* shoe industry is used to dealing with every known shape and size of foot.

Though it is unwise to wear second-hand shoes as a way of keeping down the cost of ballet training, well organized schools may arrange for sales of good quality second-hand uniforms. It is, of course, possible to make simple skirts yourself, and there is plenty of scope for knitting leg-warmers!

GENERAL GROOMING

Every dance-wear shop now stocks a fantastic range of brightly coloured dance clothes, striped leg-warmers and jazzy leotards. Fun though these may be, they are not for the young ballet student. With them the dance class becomes a show, and the leg-warmers hide badly pointed feet from the teacher's eye!

Fortunately, most schools follow the guide of the examining organizations and insist on a simple basic uniform, though nowadays there is much more variety than there has been in the past.

A dancer should always be perfectly dressed and groomed. It is part of the self-discipline which goes hand-in-hand with the ballet training itself, and is evidence of the pupil's serious approach. The most obvious points to remember are that shoes should be neat and clean and the girls' leotards and boys' tee shirts should fit correctly and comfortably.

Boys should wear their hair short. Girls should choose a neat style with long hair tied back, preferably into a bun to give a good line to the head and neck. Long fringes should be pinned back to show the face clearly, and no jewellery should be worn during the class. It distracts the teacher's eye and can prove dangerous to the others in the class.

Above left: Correct grooming of hair.
Below left: Incorrect grooming!

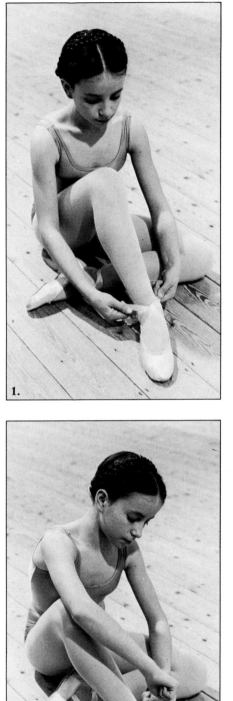

1.

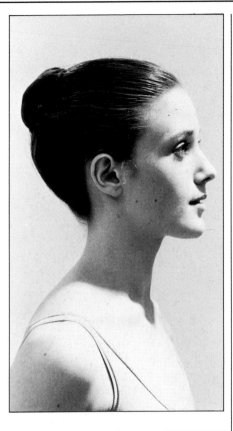

4.

HOW TO TIE THE RIBBONS

1. Cross the ribbons over in front of the ankle (satin ribbons have a special backing to prevent them from slipping).

2. Take the ribbons round behind the ankle and cross them over again.

3. Lie one on top of the other in front of the leg (not too high up).

4. Bring the ends round to the inside of the ankle and knot them tightly by the hollow next to the ankle bone.

5. To prevent the knot from slipping, wet it with a little water before tucking it, along with the ends, underneath the ribbons. The ribbon that you buy comes in a standard length. Cut the excess (approx 1″) off close to the knot in order to make a neat finish.

Bend the back of the shoe forwards against the insole. Attach the ribbon or elastic securely at the point of the fold, without sewing through the drawstring which runs round the upper edge of the shoe and which tightens this edge so that it lies close to the foot without gaping. The drawstring should be tied in a bow (not a knot as it may work loose from time to time) with the ends tucked in under the shoe.

TAKING AN EXAMINATION

It is natural to feel a little nervous before an exam. Margot Fonteyn remembers that she always had a temperature for three days before her exams, causing her family a great deal of worry, but she always seemed to recover on the day and to pass to everyone's satisfaction. If you are well prepared by your teacher for your exam you should look forward to it with excitement and anticipation.

You should remember that the examination is only a way of you and your teacher *together* seeing how you are progressing. The results are not necessarily an indication of whether or not you are going to become a professional dancer. They are just the first rungs of a very long ladder, and their aim is to set you on the upward path.

Your teacher will let you know when you are ready to take a particular exam, and it is likely that you will have had at least a year's study of a wider syllabus before you approach it, with a little extra work on the set syllabus for the exam nearer the date. Your teacher may even advise that you should take a few extra classes as the exam draws near. You can always do a little work at home by yourself, but it is best to keep this to a minimum, perhaps just refreshing your memory about the French ballet terms so that when your examiner asks for a particular step or movement you will not have to think too hard.

Your teacher will also help you to gain confidence by letting you know other details of what will be expected of you. As your teacher will have prepared many pupils for exams, he or she will let you know exactly how to enter and leave the examination room, and how to behave during the exam itself. Having a full knowledge of these facts will help you feel more comfortable and confident.

If your examination is not taking place at your own school, your teacher will almost certainly arrange for you to take a look at the new room. Then you can check to see what the floor surface is like, or if the room is an unusual shape. Try your hand on the *barre* as it might be different in some way to the one you are used to, and also notice the lighting, which might distract you. All these points will help you feel absolutely comfortable, leaving you to put all your thought and energy into your dancing.

Having the right clothes and props, such as ribbons or tambourines for character dances, for instance, is also important. When Margot Fonteyn arrived at Sadler's Wells Theatre for her first audition she did not take any practice clothes or ballet shoes, so she auditioned barefoot in her petticoat. She succeeded, but your examiner might not be so pleased with you if by any chance you did the same! Fortunately this is a worry you are unlikely to have as there will almost certainly be special rules about your uniform depending on your particular syllabus. Boys will need their regular practice clothes; girls may need a character skirt. You might be tempted to keep a new pair of shoes or a new leotard specially for the day, but this can be unwise as you could feel very uncomfortable in them. If your syllabus requires that you should wear your hair in a particular style it is a good idea to try the style out a few times in advance to make sure you can put it up securely, especially if it is very different from your usual one. If you don't, you might find that your head movements feel strange or restricted.

As you can see, all this advice is to make you feel better on the day so that you can perform naturally and with confidence. Examiners are not there to frighten you, as they have a pretty good idea of how you are feeling, and will do their best to put you at your ease, particularly as you both have something in common – a love of dancing. It's worth remembering that they are just as likely to enjoy watching a relaxed and happy dancer who has a good sense of music and performance as they are a dancer who performs all the set steps perfectly, but without feeling.

GLOSSARY OF TERMS

A

à la seconde To second position.

à terre On the ground.

adage (p.131) The part of the class where slow, flowing, controlled movements are combined to develop grace, beauty and balance.

arabesque A position in which the dancer balances on one leg with the other extended behind.

arabesque penchée An arabesque tilted over so that the back is lowered towards the floor as the stretched leg is raised up.

arrière (en) Backwards.

assemblé Assembled, or brought together.

avant (en) Forwards.

B

balancé de côté Balancer means to swing or to rock; de côté means to the side. This is a step which rocks from side to side.

barre A bar that you hold on to while doing the first part of your class (from Grade One onwards) to help you to develop strength and skill while being supported.

battement Literally translated, it means a beating movement.

battement frappé Frappé means 'struck' – the ball of the foot strikes the surface of the floor as the leg extends to an open position.

battement glissé Glissé means 'sliding' or 'gliding'. The foot slides out with enough energy to bring the toes just off the floor.

battement tendu Tendu means 'stretched'. The leg and foot are stretched away from the body – the toes remaining on the ground.

bourrée An eighteenth century dance.

bras bas Arms down. This is a position of the arms from which all other positions commence. It is also a resting position for the arms between exercises.

C

changements Springs in which you change your feet in the air.

changer To change.

ciseaux Scissors. Sometimes a *sissonne* is referred to as a *pas de ciseaux* because it resembles scissors being opened and closed.

cou-de-pied Neck of the foot, or ankle joint.

croisé (en) A direction of the body in which one side of the body is turned slightly away from the front, with the leg nearest the audience crossed in front of the other.

D

danseur noble A dancer of fine appearance.

dedans (en) Inwards.

dégagé Means to 'free, separate, disengage'. The term given to the movement of the leg and foot when it is separated or disengaged from a closed to an open position à terre.

dehors (en) Outwards.

demi-bras Half arms. A position of the arms, found halfway between the first and second positions, with the palms turned slightly upwards.

demi-pliés Half bend.

demi-pointe Half point, ie to stand on the ball of the foot.

demi-seconde Half second. A position of the arms found halfway between second position and bras bas.

derrière Behind.

devant In front.

développé To open out, unfold, develop.

E

écarté (en) Separated, or thrown apart. One leg is stretched to second position with the body turned slightly away from the audience and head turned over front shoulder.

echapper To escape.

echappé sauté A spring in which the feet escape from each other at the highest point and land in an open position.

effacé (en) A direction of the body in which one side of the body is turned slightly away from the front with the leg furthest away from the audience in front of the other.

en arrière Backwards.

en avant Forwards.

en croisé Crossed. One side of the body is turned away from the front with the leg nearest the audience crossed in front of the other.

en croix In the shape of a cross.

en dedans Inwards.

en dehors Outwards.

en écarté See écarté above.

en effacé See effacé, above.

en face To the front, facing the front.

en fondu Melted, sunk, bent.

enchaînement Enchaîner means to link and enchaînement is when two or more steps are linked together and danced to music.

en l'air In the air.

entrechat (quatre) Interweaving or braiding. A step consisting of a spring into the air making rapid beating movements with both legs. The name of the entrechat depends on the combined number of beats made by each leg, for example entrechat quatre (four), entrechat six (six).

épaulement Shouldering. A position in which one shoulder is further forward than the other.

F

face (en) Facing the front.

fondu Melted, ie sinking gently down into a bend on one leg.

frappé Beaten or struck.

full pointe Standing on the top of the toes in shoes specially made to protect them.

G

galop A travelling step, done sideways or forwards or round the outside of the room.

glissade A gliding step which serves as a preparation or as a link for others.

glissé Sliding or gliding.

grand, grande Big, large.

grand battement A movement taken at the barre and, later, in the centre, in which the leg is thrown from the hip high into the air.

grand jeté Jeter means to throw. A large leap. One leg is thrown away from the other to help lift the body and carry it along in the air.

grand plié A bending of the knees in a plié until the thighs are horizontal with the floor.

J

jeter To throw (see Grand jeté).

L

l'air (en) In the air.

O

oblique (line, of arabesque) A slanting line.

P

pas A step.

pas de bourrée Step of the bourrée, an eighteenth century dance.

pas de chat Step of a cat.

pas de cheval Step of a horse.

pas de ciseaux Step of the scissors, a name sometimes given to a sissonne (see below).

penchée Tilted or leaning over, as in an arabesque penchée, in which the leg is lifted high at the back tilting the back forwards towards the ground.

petit Little, small.

petits jetés Small springs from one leg to the other.

piqué Pricked, sharp, staccato.

pirouette A turn or a spin on one leg.

pirouette en dedans A pirouette turning inwards.

pirouette en dehors A pirouette turning outwards.

pirouette position The position in which you turn.

plié A bending of the knees.

plier To bend.

pointe, demi To stand on half point, ie on the ball of your foot.

pointe, full To stand on the top of your toes in shoes specially made to protect them.

ports de bras Carriage of the arms. There are ports de bras exercises in all grades to help you to learn how to move your arms gracefully and expressively.

posé A step.

poser To step out in any direction.

posé temps levé To step and spring into the air from one leg.

Q

quatre Four.

R

relevé Lifted or raised up.

retiré Means withdrawn. A movement in which you draw up the thigh in second position, knee bent, sliding the toes up to the side of the supporting leg until they reach the hollow at the back of the knee.

révérence A curtsey or bow.

ronds de jambe Circular movements of the leg.

S

sauté Sprung.

sauter To spring.

seconde, à la To second position.

set adage A set sequence of slow, controlled movements, practised in class in preparation for an examination.

sissonne A step of elevation, taking off from two feet and alighting on one foot (ordinaire and ouverte) or on two feet (fermée). (See ciseaux and pas de ciseaux.)

soubresaut A spring from two feet to two feet without a change, crossing one leg in front of the other in the air, so that the back foot is hidden by the front one.

T

tendu Stretched.

temps levé Raising the body by springing into the air from one leg. (p. 97)

terre (à) On the ground.

tour en l'air A spring in which you make one or more turns in the air before landing.